The Meaning of Shared Value

The concept of Creating Shared Value (CSV) – creating 'economic' value in a way that also creates value for the whole of society – has risen in prominence as a corporate policy and a strategy in recent years, mainly for third sector or development organisations. However, while it has received considerable interest among business leaders and practitioners, it has also sparked a bitter debate among academics, proponents and sceptics of the idea. Starting from this argument, the book develops a meta-critical examination of the hidden presuppositions of both supporters and critics of Creating Shared Value, particular in relation to the concept of value. It is argued that there are not two separate types of value, i.e. an economic value and a social value, but only a unique one: which essentially means the creation of well-being. If anything, the distinction that is drawn relates to the value capture (how the value created is distributed among different stakeholders) and not to value creation (additions to potential well-being), since the notion of value itself is univocal. Behind the debate are two implicit opposed viewpoints on the philosophy of history: an antagonistic (pessimistic) and a cooperative (optimistic) view. The authors are thus led to a discussion of which of the two visions appears to be the most rational in today's world. The book is addressed to readers with an interest in the core concept of value, primarily in economics, strategic management, and philosophy.

Paolo Ricci is Full Professor of Business Administration and Public Accountability at the University of Naples Federico II, Italy. He coordinated several international research projects and he is a member of numerous editorial committees. Paolo was also member of the economic policy Staff of the Italian President of the Council of Ministers (2020–2021). His research studies and publications primarily focus on corporate social responsibility, accountability and social reporting, mainly in the public sector.

Patrick O'Sullivan is Full Professor at Grenoble Ecole de Management, France. He served as Director of Studies (2006–2009) and Head of Department of People Organisations and Society (2009–2012). His research interests include Critical Scientific Methodology, Business Ethics, Transport Policy issues and System Timetabling/Planning, a field in which he has some consultancy experience.

Floriana Fusco is a post-doctoral researcher at the University of Sannio, Italy. She is a member of the scientific committee of *Mecosan* journal and a member of several national and international academic societies. Her main research fields include social responsibility and sustainability reporting, coproduction and co-creation of value, third mission and entrepreneurial universities.

The Meaning of Shared Value

New Perspective on Creating Shared Value

Paolo Ricci, Patrick O'Sullivan and Floriana Fusco

Routledge
Taylor & Francis Group

LONDON AND NEW YORK

First published 2024
by Routledge
4 Park Square, Milton Park, Abingdon, Oxon OX14 4RN

and by Routledge
605 Third Avenue, New York, NY 10158

Routledge is an imprint of the Taylor & Francis Group, an informa business

© 2024 Paolo Ricci, Patrick O'Sullivan and Floriana Fusco

The right of Paolo Ricci, Patrick O'Sullivan and Floriana Fusco to be identified as authors of this work has been asserted in accordance with sections 77 and 78 of the Copyright, Designs and Patents Act 1988.

British Library Cataloguing-in-Publication Data
A catalogue record for this book is available from the British Library

Library of Congress Cataloging-in-Publication Data
Names: Fusco, Floriana, author. | Ricci, Paolo (Professor of business administration) author. | O'Sullivan, Patrick, 1951– author.
Title: The meaning of shared value : new perspective on creating shared value / Floriana Fusco, Paolo Ricci and Patrick O'Sullivan.
Description: 1 Edition. | New York : Routledge, 2024. |
Series: Routledge Frontiers of Political Economy |
Includes bibliographical references and index. |
Identifiers: LCCN 2023014860 (print) | LCCN 2023014861 (ebook) |
ISBN 9781032505428 (hardback) | ISBN 9781003398943 (ebook)
Subjects: LCSH: Value. | Economic value added.
Classification: LCC HB201 .F87 2024 (print) | LCC HB201 (ebook) |
DDC 335.4/12–dc23/eng/20230330
LC record available at https://lccn.loc.gov/2023014860
LC ebook record available at https://lccn.loc.gov/2023014861

ISBN: 9781032505428 (hbk)
ISBN: 9781032505459 (pbk)
ISBN: 9781003398943 (ebk)

DOI: 10.4324/9781003398943

Typeset in Times New Roman
by Newgen Publishing UK

Contents

1 Introduction

Recent years have witnessed a remarkably heated controversy in the management theory literature between those who have lined up as defenders and opponents of Creating Shared Value (CSV). Well, the purpose of this book is not to delve into the niceties of the arguments on offer or to add more fuel to the flames of discord. Instead, it is to engage in a meta-critique of some of the concepts involved and the implicit philosophical presuppositions that underlie the positions adopted on both sides. These can shed some interesting light on the debate and may help bemused spectators find their way through the controversy and some of the events shaping our time. We will argue in particular that while CSV may not be particularly original as a concept in the Corporate Social Responsibility (CSR)/Business Ethics literature (it clearly draws inspiration from stakeholder theory and even social contract theories, for example), nonetheless, an examination of its philosophical roots reveals a refreshingly novel perspective on human affairs. Drawing on economic theory, philosophy, and managerial literature, our argumentation shows that at the core of the controversy, there lies a fundamental confusion, shared by both sides, about the notion of value itself. We would propose that the dichotomy which appears to be common to all protagonists in the CSV debate – and not only – between 'economic value' and 'social value' is entirely false and a source of considerable misunderstanding since it has not to do with the creation of value, but with its capture. Delving beneath this debate and related criticisms reverberating between the two sides will also lead us to detect two fundamentally opposing views of the philosophy of history: an antagonistic versus a collaborative

DOI: 10.4324/9781003398943-1

view of the evolution of human affairs, with some corollary, critical reflections, including a recalibration of the notion of rationality as used (or abused) by economists, and applied by companies.

The relevance of the debate on the value that companies should create (which value? for whom?) is an ever-current topic (see Figure 1.1, featuring a collage of recent newspaper articles).

However, if up to 50 years ago it was commonly accepted that the company had to make (only) money, this belief has gradually begun to waver in academic spheres before institutional and corporate ones. This trend became irrepressible after the great financial crisis that started in 2008. The capitalist system was challenged as never before; to use Porter and Kramer's words, it 'is under siege' (Porter & Kramer, 2011, p. 62). No one has tended to deny capitalism's merit in generating wealth and economic development. Instead, as never before, there has been questioning about its defects, including its intrinsic instability and ethical foundations. What is the (environmental, for example) cost of industrial revolutions in the Asian Tigers? To what extent are the inequalities it brings with it tolerable? (Plender, 2015; Stiglitz, 2012). Therefore, what the great crisis did was to pull down the curtain on the limits of market triumphalism and the conception according to which everything can be put up for sale and, in parallel, it can be bought (Sandel, 2013). It should be noted that the wave of discontent or, at least, of perplexity has concerned not only companies but also institutions, i.e. the public political actor, who has firmly pushed towards that model, progressively abdicating its regulation and correction functions, as well as perpetuating a dubious deficit reduction strategy, called austerity.

The challenges of climate change and the Covid-19 pandemic have again raised questions about many of these same presuppositions regarding the role of the company in society (we argue in Chapter 3 that firms cannot be considered other than as being in society, being itself a social actor); and regarding the role of the state (government) in the economy.

Leaving aside the question of the public actor and focusing on the business side, the thrust is to develop a conception of business that goes beyond the traditional model and rethink the purpose of business so that it is interconnected with normative values and ethics, as well as profit (Freeman et al., 2020). 'It is about solving problems, "to produce profitable solutions to the problems of people

Figure 1.1 Collage of recent newspaper articles on the concept of value in business.

Source: Authors' elaboration from newspaper articles.

and planet" and "not to profit from producing problems for people or planet"' (Mayer, 2021, p. 897). There have been many proposals for new business models, including CSV. Businesses, at least formally, seem to back some of these novel ideas, as demonstrated by the recent 'Statement on the Purpose of a Corporation' published in August 2019 by Business Roundtable,[1] which is the Gotha of American capitalism (e.g. Apple, Amazon, Coca-Cola). In addition to confirming the need for generating long-term value for shareholders, the Statement declares the commitment to deliver value to all stakeholders 'for the future success of our companies, our communities and our country'. Even in this case, the reactions have been numerous, including copious sceptical responses from those who saw in the Statement yet another greenwashing campaign. Indeed, if it is unquestionable that there are many driving forces behind the change, the news that reaches us every day is still not free from reports of corporate scandals and critical situations. So, it seems premature to draw definitive and assertive conclusions about the practical results of this long and ongoing process, especially taking into account that, in the meantime, other and further changes are characterising the capitalist system (e.g. the growing importance of big data), which will undoubtedly bring about new opportunities, but also new (ethical) dilemmas.

Resolving these questions of contemporary business sincerity and motivation will not be our goal. Rather, starting from a specific controversy on CSV, we want to offer a philosophical exegesis or hermeneutics of the concept of value as used across a variety of disciplines with a view to clarifying some of the confusion that to us appears to generate misunderstandings regarding a term which is so widely bandied around but so often at cross purposes, namely value. Through a critical reflection, we will also seek to uncover the implicit presuppositions inherent in the theoretical positions adopted by various economics and management theorists. At the end of the five short chapters (Figure 1.2 summarises the conceptual map of the book), the readers may not have a certain answer on what the future of corporations will be. However, we hope they will have more straightforward ideas on how to interpret the present and what could be the most advantageous choice (which is not certain to be the chosen one). However, it is worth emphasising that the company is praxis, a human-sensitive activity. Therefore, the possibility of overthrowing today's system (or those to

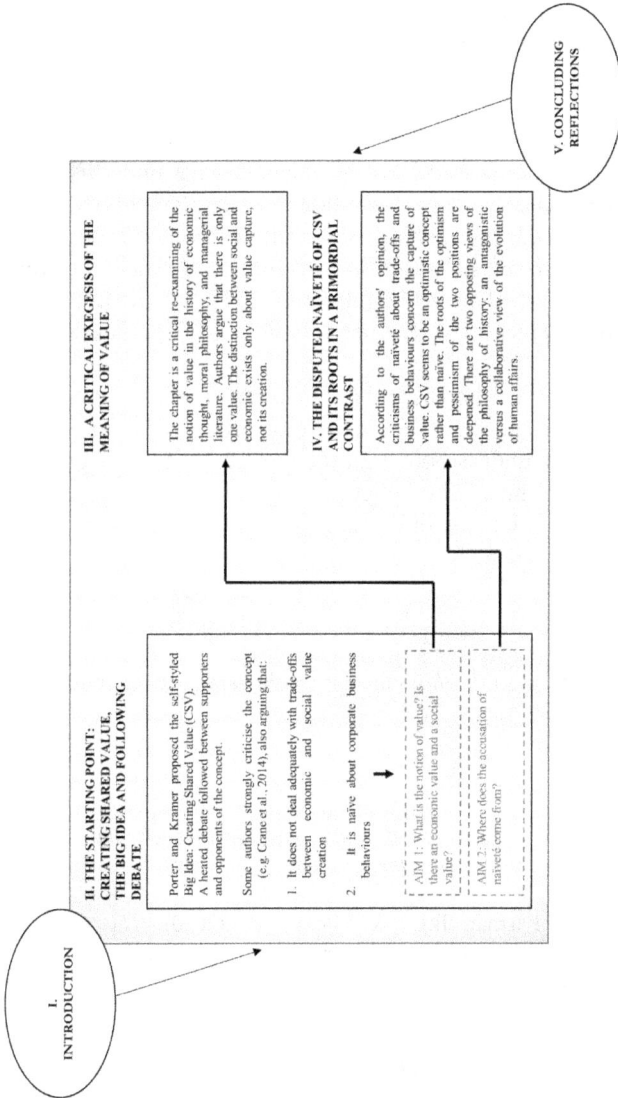

Figure 1.2 Conceptual map of the book.

Source: Authors' elaboration.

come) depends on the actions of the individuals, which in turn are, above all, initiatives based on thought (Masullo & Ricci, 2015).

The book's originality lies in the Keynes/Myrdal-inspired elucidation of hidden and probably entirely unconscious preconceptions and resulting confusion regarding the term 'value' in management and economics literature and, in particular, in the debates over CSV together with a critical reflection on their philosophical roots.

In this regard, we would point out that a succession of leading thinkers in Economics and Social Sciences have underlined the importance of clearly stating the hidden value judgments (Myrdal, 1959) and, indeed, the ideological presuppositions (Dobb, 1973) and/or human interests which are inevitably prevalent in every attempt to theorise the world (Habermas, 1972). Above all, in this context, we may recall J.M. Keynes's (1936, p. 241) famous remark,

> [The ideas of] economists and political philosophers, both when they are right and when they are wrong, are more powerful than is commonly understood. Indeed, the world is ruled by little else. Practical men, who believe themselves to be quite exempt from any intellectual influences, are usually slaves of some defunct economist.

Note

1 Retrieved from https://opportunity.businessroundtable.org/ourcom mitment/, on 29 August 2019.

References

Dobb, M. (1973). *Theories of value and distribution since Adam Smith: ideology and economic theory*. Cambridge: Cambridge University Press.

Freeman, R.E., Parmar, B.L., & Martin, K. (2020). *The power of and: responsible business without trade-offs*. New York: Columbia University Press.

Habermas, J. (1972). *Knowledge and human interests* (1st English ed.). Boston, MA: Beacon Press.

Keynes, J.M. (1936). *The general theory of employment interest and money*. London: Palgrave Macmillan.

Masullo, A., & Ricci, P. (2015). *Tempo della vita e mercato del tempo. Dialoghi tra filosofia ed economia sul tempo: verso una critica dell'azienda capitalistica*. Milan: FrancoAngeli.

Mayer, C. (2021). The future of the corporation and the economics of purpose. *Journal of Management Studies*, *58*(3), 887–901.

Myrdal, G. (1959). *Value in social theory*. London: Routledge.

Plender, J. (2015). *Capitalism: money, morals and markets*. London: Biteback Publishing.

Porter, M.E., & Kramer, M. (2011). Creating Shared Value. *Harvard Business Review*, *89*(1), 62–77.

Sandel, M.J. (2013). *What money can't buy: the moral limits of markets*. London: Penguin.

Stiglitz, J.E. (2012). *The price of inequality: how today's divided society endangers our future*. New York: W.W. Norton.

2 The starting point

Creating Shared Value, the Big Idea, and the following debate

2.1 The self-styled 'Big Idea': Creating Shared Value

In 2011 the leading business strategy theorists Michael Porter and Mark Kramer published an article (Porter & Kramer, 2011) that was to prove highly influential and – surprisingly – controversial. The article proposed the self-styled 'Big Idea': Creating Shared Value (CSV), defined as 'policies and operating practices that enhance the competitiveness of a company while simultaneously advancing the economic and social conditions in the communities in which it operates' (Porter & Kramer, 2011, p. 67). As they note, 'the capitalist system is under siege', and 'the legitimacy of business has fallen to levels not seen in recent history'. They stress that paradoxically 'the more business has begun to embrace corporate social responsibility, the more it has been blamed for society's failures' (Porter & Kramer, 2011, p. 64). On this point, however, a few annotations must be made. The term 'creating shared value' was initially coined by Porter and Kramer in the early 2000s in a series of articles in the *Harvard Business Review*, first on competitive advantage and corporate philanthropy (e.g. Porter & Kramer, 2002) and then, more detailed, in the article 'The link between Competitive Advantage and Corporate Social Responsibility', in which they promoted a strategic and non-philanthropic approach to Corporate Social Responsibility (CSR) as a possible source of competitive advantage (Porter & Kramer, 2006). Five years later, going beyond their own earlier article, they proposed to supersede the concept of CSR, arguing that in the face of the post-2008 crisis of capitalism, 'the solution lies in the principle of shared value which involves creating economic value in a

DOI: 10.4324/9781003398943-2

way that also creates value for society by addressing its needs and challenges' (Porter & Kramer, 2011, p. 64). According to the authors, CSV allows for overcoming the traditional trade-off between economic efficiency and social progress, or, in other words, between societal benefits and companies' economic success. This is because it is based on the assumption that, on the one hand, companies must aim at long-term success; on the other hand, there are points of intersection between companies and society's needs, which generate mutually beneficial markets. These points of intersection are those societal matters that may also be good business opportunities. There are three main key ways through which companies can seize these opportunities for creating shared value: (i) reconceiving products and markets (i.e. refocusing the proposition on the real – and unmet – needs of consumers and their well-being, such as healthy nutrition); (ii) redefining productivity in the value chain (i.e. modify the value chain taking into account that negative externalities create social costs but often also lead to an increase in costs for the company, as in the case of excessive packaging); (iii) enabling local cluster development (i.e. improve context conditions for clusters, trying to address weaknesses – such as institutional or educational – and cooperating with local stakeholders).

Case example 2.1 Creating Shared Value at Nestlé

Nestlé is the first organisation to formally adopt a CSV strategy (Nestlé CSV report, 2011). Since 2006, it has intentionally identified opportunities for integrating economic and social needs by focusing on three areas of concern for the company –nutrition, water and rural development.

Investigating the nutrition area, Nestlé has realised the severe health problems caused by the deficiency of micronutrients, including iron, for people living in poverty across the globe. For more than 100 years, Nestlé has served customers in developing and emerging markets with its Maggi seasonings and other Popularly Positioned Products (PPPs). Hence it identified the social need to reduce iron deficiency as a potential opportunity for its business. Specifically, it started evaluating a strategy of reconceiving products and markets, being willing first to renew and then innovate its products. This process led the Corporate Wellness Unit specialists to choose bouillon cubes in Nigeria as a prime product renovation candidate. Since the product had very high popularity and awareness (that is, high sales), the challenge was to increase the level of iron without changing the flavour, colour, and cost, as consumers are very sensitive to price variation. The teamwork, which lasted two years, between the Nestlé manager of the Nigerian company and the Corporate Wellness, Sales and Marketing, and R&D units, managed to identify a nut formula that contained more iron, had a similar colour and taste and managed to find a cost-neutral solution for the Nigerian population, offering a different solution for the different local conditions. Despite the risks, this gamble paid off: sales remained solid and Nigerian consumers took in more iron.

Sources: Adaptation from Crutchfield et al. (2013). Built to Create Shared Value: how Nestlé tackles malnutrition in developing regions, FSG & SVI case study, retrieved from www.sharedvalue.org/resource/nestle-sha red-value-case-study-in-micronutrient-fortification/; Nestlé (2011). Nestlé Creating Shared Value report 2011, retrieved from www.nestle.com/sites/ default/files/asset-library/documents/library/documents/corporate_social_ responsibility/2011-csv-report.pdf

Although the topic will not be deepened here, but in the following chapters, it should be emphasised that Porter and Kramer explicitly state that CSV does not concern a different redistribution of value but the creation of greater value, both economic and social. As an example, the article compares the fair trade movement, which increases the revenues of poor farmers by paying them higher prices for the same crops, and a CSV strategy, which would consist in finding new solutions, such as an improvement of current techniques and a strengthening of the local cluster. This would generate an increase in farmers' efficiency, yields, product quality, and sustainability, and so in the revenues and profits of both farmers and the companies that buy from them.

Although the concept is envisioned for the for-profit sector, the authors point out that it can also be applied in the public and non-profit sectors. Furthermore, it is worth emphasising, especially considering what will be said in the following paragraphs and chapters, that they imagine a key role for the government. First of all, it should be noted that the CSV assumes, like the CSR, compliance with the law. Second, the authors emphasise the role of regulation in promoting CSV: 'The right kind of government regulation can encourage companies to pursue shared value; the wrong kind works against it and even makes trade-offs between economic and social goals inevitable' (p. 74). Among this '*right* regulation', they mention the presence of clear and measurable social goals, performance standards, and universal measurement and performance reporting systems. According to the authors, it is better to avoid regulations that force compliance or inflict costs on companies because this may increase resistance and an old mindset. In contrast, the widespread and progressive acceptance of the CSV concept will lead companies to align themselves with the 'right regulation' increasingly.

The idea has received considerable interest among business leaders and practitioners – especially in the wake of the ravages of the 2008 financial crisis – and it has been a significant practical influence in the approach to strategy formation in some companies (e.g. Nestlé) and third-sector or development organisations (e.g. International Finance Corporation-IFC). However, it has been less successful among academics, to the point that we can say that the most recent literature is indifferent, if not oblivious, to the CSV concept. For instance, in recent special issues/symposia on CSR of some leading journals, the Porter Kramer CSV approach is not even mentioned or referenced (e.g. *Academy of Management Journal* Thematic Issue, in 2016, *Journal of Business Ethics* thematic symposium on Emerging Paradigms of CSR, in 2019, or Society for Business Ethics Conference, linked to *Business Ethics Quarterly*, in 2022). This is also evident from a quick comparison between the number of documents published on CSV compared to those published on the more traditional and accepted CSR concept between 2011 and to present. Entering,[1] in the database Scopus, the query 'corporate social responsibility' in 'title, abstract, keywords' on 29 December 2022 and refining the search by time (2011–to present), 23,117 documents resulted. The number drops to 305 entering the query 'creating shared value'; the amount changes by inserting less restrictive keywords like 'shared value' (n. 3,052).

Hence, from a theoretical point of view, if the concept was taken up enthusiastically by some academic commentators (e.g. Moon et al., 2011; Spitzeck & Chapman, 2012), it also has been openly and strongly criticised by numerous academics (e.g. Elkington, 2011; Aakhus & Bzdak, 2012; Beschorner, 2014; Crane et al., 2014). Between the two extreme positions, it must be emphasised that there are other intermediate (e.g. de los Reyes et al., 2017; Corazza et al., 2017; de los Reyes & Scholz, 2019). It also appears that many scholars and practitioners do not distinguish the two concepts (CSR/CSV) and, rather than alternatives, consider them consequential or complementary (for instance, Roszkowska-Menkes, 2018).

It is necessary to underline that in the continuum of CSV debate, the positions taken are not always so clear-cut, and some criticisms raised by the opponents' side (e.g. non-novelty) are also present among those who hold opinions in favour of constructive criticism. What changes, however, is the general sentiment towards the concept and the consideration that it may or may not contribute to the theoretical and practical debate on the relationship between business and society.[2]

2.2 The opponents' position and the main criticisms of CSV

As mentioned in the previous paragraph, the final development and the launch of the 'Big Idea' was followed by a broad and open debate, heated by manifold positions. Among these, the well-known business ethics theorists Crane et al. (2014) have elaborated the most scathing critique of the CSV approach. In fact, while on the one hand, they recognise some of CSV's strengths, including the great appeal for corporations and the consideration of social goals at the strategic level, on the other hand, they stress multiple weaknesses, arguing that it is naïvely optimistic and fails to face up to the more difficult challenges of a comprehensive effort at CSR by businesses. CSV, they say, 'is unoriginal, it ignores the tensions between social and economic goals, it is naïve about the challenges of business compliance, and it is based on a shallow conception of the role of the corporation in society' (Crane et al., 2014, p. 131). With regard to the first critique, namely the lack of originality, they argue that in portraying CSR as having been considered separately from the core business, Porter and Kramer

ignore decades of (strategic) literature and bind it to mere philanthropy (Crane et al., 2014). In effect, Porter and Kramer cari-
cature about 70 years of scientific literature.[3] Without pretending
to retrace the whole long evolutionary journey of the concept
of Corporate Social Responsibility here, we mention some of
the early definitions – such as Carroll (1979, p. 500): 'The social
responsibility of business encompasses the economic, legal, ethical
and discretionary expectations that society has of organisations at
a given point in time' or Drucker's (1984) first foundation of strategic CSR, according to which 'the proper "social responsibility"
of business is to tame the dragon, that is to turn a social problem
into economic opportunity and economic benefit, into productive
capacity, into human competence, into well-paid jobs, and into
wealth' (p. 62). In the managerial literature of recent years, we
can find a gradual and progressive appreciation of the strategic
implication of CSR. For example, in 2001, McWilliams and Siegel
determined an 'ideal' level of CSR, which made it neutral with
respect to financial performance and defined CSR 'as actions that
appear to further some social good, beyond the interests of the
firm and that which is required by law' (2001, p. 117),[4] later they
specifically define strategic CSR 'as any "responsible" activity
that allows a firm to achieve a sustainable competitive advantage, regardless of motive' (2011, p. 1481). Yet another prominent
author, i.e. Lantos (2001), explicitly talks about strategic CSR as a
win-win situation for company and stakeholders and asserts 'that
much of the uncertainty about the legitimacy and domain of CSR
stems from failure to distinguish the ethical and philanthropic
dimensions as well as from the misguided notion that it is somehow
objectionable for business to prosper from good works (what I call
"strategic CSR")' (p. 596). The same Porter and Kramer in 2006
stress the need to shift towards a strategic approach to CSR, which
'moves beyond good corporate citizenship and mitigating harmful
value chain impacts to mount a small number of initiatives whose
social and business benefits are large and distinctive' (p. 10).

From what has been written, it must not even be understood
that all the literature on CSR places the accent on its strategic
nature. Many are the conceptualisations and theories on CSR (see,
for example, Garriga & Melé, 2004) and, consequently, there has
been considerable ambiguity about the exact meaning of CSR
and its link to business strategy. So, if, on the one hand, this puts

into perspective the criticisms moved by Crane et al., on the other hand, it leads to consider that when Porter and Kramer take aim at CSR, they are shooting at a rather ambiguous moving target. An unacknowledged debt is also highlighted by Crane et al. and other scholars (Beschorner, 2014; Dembek et al., 2016) with reference to stakeholder management and social innovation literature. According to Aakhus and Bzdak (2012), CSV also has some similarities with the concept of Blended Value Proposition (Emerson, 2003), Stuart Hart's (2005) book, *Capitalism at the Crossroads: The unlimited business opportunities in solving the world's most difficult problems*, or with the concept of sustainability (Bruntland, 1987; Elkington, 1997, 1998). The criticism of lack of originality and theoretical deficiency is certainly the one that has been most advanced against CSV, and it has been suggested that it is a 'management buzzword' rather than a substantive theoretical concept (Dembek et al., 2016). In summary, it could be said that if CSV certainly has the merit of emphasising the need for a strategic and long-term vision that goes well beyond purely philanthropic behaviour (Esposito & Ricci, 2016), it may not, in the end, be particularly original in the CSR/Business Ethics literature. In addition, one could even see a linkage between CSV and the much more ancient social contract theories of the state as expounded by political philosophers, but more of that later.

The second line of Crane and colleagues' criticism is related to the lack of consideration of the trade-offs that may be generated between the creation of economic and social value. To quote Aakhus and Bzdak (2012, p. 235), 'what is problematic with SVM [shared value model] lies less with what it highlights about the business society relationship and more with what it hides'. Crane et al. (2014), in fact, reproach Porter and Kramer for dwelling only on win-win situations, whereas most of the circumstances, in reality, reveal themselves in the form of a dilemma, where one or more parties are 'losers'. And this is regardless of the good intentions of corporations and especially in cases of global supply chains (think of the Nike scandals).[5] The 'selective focus' on a win-win situation leads Crane et al. (2014) to state that 'while CSV might be a good way of integrating various activities into one social strategy, it fails to deliver orientation for a responsible corporate-wide strategy. It thus fails in Porter and Kramer's aim to redefine the purpose of the corporation.' (p. 139).

The third criticism is that of naïveté, due to the excessive optimism with which the 'fathers' of the CSV concept hypothesise ('presume') the compliance of companies with the law and regulations. On this point, in truth, Porter and Kramer, in stating that a very stringent regulation could, in any case, generate resistance and persistence of an old companies' mentality, seem to want to imply the possibility of non-compliant behaviour. The same when they state, 'regulation will be needed to limit the pursuit of exploitative, unfair, or deceptive practices in which companies benefit at the expense of society.' (Porter & Kramer, 2011, p. 74). Rather, in our opinion, a certain optimism would appear to be there when they say that the progressive acceptance of the CSV concept will lead to progressive self-regulation in many areas. Furthermore, on the other hand, they are not the only ones to have uneasy feelings about stringent regulation in these areas. Looking at the CSR side, de Colle et al. (2014) have highlighted how CSR standards can lead to some paradoxes, including the tendency to develop a thoughtless, quasi-automatic mindset, according to which behaviour does not derive from an evaluation of what would be more right/responsible, but merely from a legalistic compliance.

Finally, Crane et al. (2014) recognise as a fourth weakness of CSV its failure to move beyond a corporate-centric vision and, therefore, to really challenge the current model of capitalism. A similar observation may also be found, for instance, in Aakhus and Bzdak (2012). Moreover, proposing the CSV as a solution to the legitimacy crisis of the current capitalist system would be a 'purely efficiency-oriented answer to a widely normative question' (Crane et al., 2014, p. 141). On the same point, Beschorner (2014) states without holds barred that 'the authors approach the topic with an overly narrow economic perspective and, as Paul Simon sang, this "one trick is all that horse can do". As a consequence, the shared value perspective regards companies as players with the ability to calculate benefits, but they cannot be conceptualised as actors beyond the economic ideology. This is both normatively inadequate and empirically wrong.' (p. 108).

2.3 The defenders of CSV

Porter and Kramer must undoubtedly be mentioned among the first – and most determined – defenders of the concept of CSV.

Indeed, without going into detail, it must be mentioned that the authors of the 'Big Idea' responded to the thorough and extensive criticism of Crane and colleagues by partially admitting the similarity with some concepts (e.g. blended value) while reaffirming the innovativeness of the CSV, and rejecting the charge of naivety, by declaring that 'legal compliance and a narrow sense of social responsibility are prerequisites to creating shared value, but the concept of shared value takes company behaviour much further' (Porter & Kramer, 2014, in 'A response to Andrew Crane et al.'s article by Michael E. Porter and Mark R. Kramer', which follows Crane et al.'s article, p. 150). Furthermore, they reverse the criticism against Crane of not grasping reality if he thinks companies can broadly engage in CSR without an economic return.

To keep them company, a number of scholars recognise CSV's innovative and powerful character while outlining some weaknesses, mainly theoretical, and therefore the need for refinement. In 2011, by quite enthusiastically welcoming the 'Big Idea', Moon and colleagues stated: 'the concept of CSV is innovative and the strategic guidelines mentioned above are very useful' (p. 52), or, again, 'scholars as well as practitioners have struggled with the concept of CSR and its strategies. Porter and Kramer have provided the answer: it is not CSR, but CSV' (p. 62). However, they have also highlighted some limits they have tried to overcome with what they define as theoretical and practical advances. Precisely, they classify corporations by considering different degrees of corporate and social benefits and propose four strategies for effectively reaching CSV. Beyond the specific content of this advancement, for which reference is made to the article in question, it is essential to underline that in categorising companies, the authors separate the CSR strategy from that of the CSV entirely, thus embracing the position of Porter and Kramer. Actually, Moon partially modified this opinion a few years later, introducing the concept of Corporate Social Opportunity (CSO) and emphasising how CSV is the 'process to reach CSO from CSR' (Moon & Parc, 2019, p. 120).

Hence, according to this side of the debate, CSV, while presenting some theoretical gaps and needs for further operationalisations, constitutes a highly pioneering idea that allows for overcoming CSR and related concepts. In fact, beyond the areas of overlap that some authors also underline (e.g. von Liel, 2016; Moon et al., 2011), it presents undeniable elements of uniqueness, including the positive relationship between economic and social performance. In this direction, Wójcik (2016, p. 33) argues that CSV 'differs conceptually from CSR in that it unifies different notions under the umbrella concept of CSR by underlining that social engagement must be economically beneficial for a company and by relating it to strategic analysis. ... Its biggest contribution is that CSV sees business activity through the lens of value creation in two dimensions: economic and social.'

Put to the test, CSV seems to work, as empirical research shows (e.g. Spitzeck & Chapman, 2012; von Liel, 2016; Alberti & Benfanti, 2019). Above all, it should be reiterated that the concept has proved to be very appealing to corporations, advisors, and consultants, as demonstrated by the development of the Shared Value Initiative (SVI), which is 'a global community of practice committed to driving adoption and implementation of shared value strategies among leading companies, civil society, and government organisations'. SVI is an initiative of FSG, and among its community, it boasts partners such as Walmart, Enel, Nestlé, Novo Nordisk, and many other big corporations.[6] In this sense, it can be said that the defenders' side is mainly animated by practitioners and academics who focus on empirical studies or try to operationalise and measure the concept of CSV. In contrast, the largest wall of criticism comes from academics who focus on the theoretical aspects.

2.4 The middle position: cautious enthusiasm and constructive criticism

Already from what was said in the previous paragraph, it can be understood that in between the strenuous defence of Porter and Kramer and the strong rejection of the whole approach by Crane et al., most of the authors have adopted a middle position, characterised by cautious enthusiasm and constructive criticism (e.g. Hartman & Werhane, 2013; Dembek et al., 2016; Mühlbacher & Böbel, 2019).

Among these positions, it is interesting to mention for the purpose of this book, Hartman and Werhane (2013), which 'are in substantial agreement with Porter and Kramer's discussion in what *Harvard Business Review* calls its "Big Idea" section' and 'share a commitment to the concept that economic value is linked to social value rather than traditional philanthropy, and thus, that social and economic progress are better served when tied to shared incentives and healthy competition' (p. 37), however, they claim to deviate from this idea on three points. The first one is the notion of profit. According to these authors, it could be argued that CSV consists of more profits for more stakeholders.

Constructive criticism is also advanced by de los Reyes et al. (2017), who try to get out of the impasse and balance the opposing positions. They argue that CSV is a robust (managerial) framework in win-win cases (cases A) but presents some weakness in win-lose cases (cases B), that is when social and business interests diverge. Hence, they propose a CSV+ framework, according to which managers should refer to a norm-taking framework or, if missing, contribute to engaging in a norm-making process when case B arises. However, the same authors take on a more critical perspective a few years later. In 2019, while reaffirming that CSV provides a 'valuable toolkit', de los Reyes and Scholz (2019) found that CSV leads to incremental innovations, failing instead in the transformative purpose, i.e. generating radical changes and innovations needed to face such problems as the climate emergency. More specifically, they argue that: (i) empirical examples of CSV can be mainly categorised as 'harm-reducing' or 'giving-back' strategies; (ii) by not questioning the premises behind legacy businesses and consisting of optimising strategies, CSV is compatible with destructive trade-offs; (iii) although CSV provides a 'useful strategy framework that stimulates optimising innovation' (p. 792), it fails to generate transformative innovation that can extinguish environmentally destructive businesses.

Other scholars added the concept to the existing ones, defining it as a 'modification of the classic CSR' (Liczmańska-Kopcewicz et al., 2019, p. 3), an 'incremental scientific development' (Menghwar & Daood, 2021, p. 481) or its direct consequence, without any risk of conflict. On the other hand, the same consequentiality is highlighted by Corazza et al. (2017) in analysing 87 reports of 29 international organisations that approached CSV practices. They found that reporting for CSV links it with CSR-related concepts and existing paradigms. Hence 'CSV-related disclosure is not creating a new reality, but only interpreting CSR-related concepts in a new way. In that sense, the new way invoked in the definition of CSV is more addressed to a managerial mindset of approaching business for society rather than a real shift to something completely different.' (p. 429).

2.5 What about our perspective?

The present study does not intend to comprehensively deepen the arguments raised by the two CSV's sides, nor the related concepts (e.g. CSR). Neither does it intend to take a position for or against. As pointed out in the introduction, this heated debate has drawn our attention to what we believe to be two crucial points that underpin it and to which we intend to offer clarification: (i) the basic notion of value itself and the alleged trade-offs between economic and social value; (ii) the naïve optimism said to underlie creating shared value.

Regarding the first point, the arguments reported in this chapter show that both sides consider two types of value (there is, therefore, agreement on this). In contrast, the clash is on which framework (CSR or CSV) best considers the trade-offs generated between them. We deem it worthwhile to offer a different point of view, which passes through a careful and critical examination of the concept of value to suggest that the notion of value is univocal.

Regarding the second point, the study will provide a philosophical interpretation of the two positions that we can define as optimistic or pessimistic about companies' compliance with the law and regulations.

Notes

1 It should be noted that the query was inserted to give an indicative count of the number of publications. Therefore, the database has not been cleaned up to eliminate the articles which, although having the term in the topic, are not focused on it.
2 Interesting and recent reviews and syntheses of theoretical positions and empirical investigations on the CSV are carried out by Menghwar, P.S., & Daood, A. (2021). Creating shared value: a systematic review, synthesis and integrative perspective. *International Journal of Management Reviews*, *23*(4), 466–85 and Dembek, K., Singh, P., & Bhakoo, V. (2016). Literature review of shared value: a theoretical concept or a management buzzword? *Journal of Business Ethics*, *137*(2), 231–67.

3 On the evolution of the concept of corporate social responsibility, see, among others: Carroll, A.B. (1999). Corporate social responsibility evolution of a definitional construct. *Business & Society, 38*(3), 268–95; Aguinis, A., & Glavas, A., (2012). What we know and don't know about corporate social responsibility: a review and research agenda. *Journal of Management, 38*(4), 932–68.
4 Authors explicitly refer to some examples which show that these actions refer to the core business and not philanthropic activities (e.g. progressive human resource management programs, developing non-animal testing procedures, recycling, abating pollution).
5 On the topic, see, for example, DeTienne, K.B., & Lewis, L.W. (2005). The pragmatic and ethical barriers to corporate social responsibility disclosure: the Nike case. *Journal of Business Ethics, 60,* 359–76; Locke, R.M. (2003). The promise and perils of globalisation: the case of Nike. *Management: Inventing and Delivering Its Future, 39,* 40.
6 Please refer to the official site of SVI: https://wwany.org/

References

Aakhus, M., & Bzdak, M. (2012). Revisiting the role of 'shared value' in the business-society relationship. *Business and Professional Ethics Journal, 31*(2), 231–6.

Aguinis, A., & Glavas, A. (2012). What we know and don't know about corporate social responsibility: a review and research agenda. *Journal of Management, 38*(4), 932–68.

Alberti, F.G., & Belfanti, F. (2019). Creating shared value and clusters: the case of an Italian cluster initiative in food waste prevention. *Competitiveness Review: An International Business Journal, 29*(1), 39–60.

Beschorner, T. (2014). Creating shared value: the one-trick pony approach. *Business Ethics Journal Review, 1*(17), 106–12.

Bruntland, G.E. (Ed.) (1987). *Our common future: the World Commission on Environment and Development.* Oxford: Oxford University Press.

Carroll, A.B. (1979). A three-dimensional conceptual model of corporate performance. *Academy of Management Review, 4*(4), 497–505.

Carroll, A.B. (1999). Corporate social responsibility evolution of a definitional construct. *Business & Society, 38*(3), 268–95.

Corazza, L., Scagnelli, S.D., & Mio, C. (2017). Simulacra and sustainability disclosure: analysis of the interpretative models of creating shared value. *Corporate Social Responsibility and Environmental Management, 24*(5), 414–34.

Crane, A., Palazzo, G., Spence, L.J., & Matten, D. (2014). Contesting the value of 'creating shared value'. *California Management Review, 56*(2), 130–53.

Crutchfield, L., Bakule, J., & Pfitzer, M. (2013). Built to create shared value: how Nestlé tackles malnutrition in developing regions. *FSG & SVI case study*. Retrieved from www.sharedvalue.org/resource/nestle-shared-value-case-study-in-micronutrient-fortification/

de Colle, S., Henriques, A., & Sarasvathy, S. (2014). The paradox of corporate social responsibility standards. *Journal of Business Ethics*, 125, 177–91.

de los Reyes Jr, G., & Scholz, M. (2019). The limits of the business case for sustainability: don't count on 'Creating Shared Value' to extinguish corporate destruction. *Journal of Cleaner Production*, *221*, 785–94.

de los Reyes Jr, G., Scholz, M., & Smith, N. C. (2017). Beyond the 'win-win' creating shared value requires ethical frameworks. *California Management Review*, *59*(2), 142–67.

Dembek, K., Singh, P., & Bhakoo, V. (2016). Literature review of shared value: a theoretical concept or a management buzzword? *Journal of Business Ethics*, *137*(2), 231–67.

DeTienne, K.B., & Lewis, L.W. (2005). The pragmatic and ethical barriers to corporate social responsibility disclosure: the Nike case. *Journal of Business Ethics*, *60*, 359–76.

Drucker, P.F. (1984). Converting social problems into business opportunities: the new meaning of corporate social responsibility. *California Management Review*, *26*(2), 53–63.

Elkington, J. (1997). *Cannibals with forks: the triple bottom line of 21st century business*. Stony Creek, CT: New Society Publishers.

Elkington, J. (1998). Partnerships from cannibals with forks: the triple bottom line of 21st-century business. *Environmental Quality Management*, *8*(1), 37–51.

Elkington, J. (2011). Don't abandon CSR for creating shared value just yet. *The Guardian*, 25 May. Retrieved from www.theguardian.com/sustainable-business/sustainability-with-john-elkington/corporate-social-resposibility-creating-shared-value

Emerson, J. (2003). The blended value proposition: integrating social and financial returns. *California Management Review*, *45*(4), 35–51.

Esposito, P., & Ricci, P. (2016). Entry 'Corporate Social Responsibility'. In A. Farazmand (Ed.), *Global encyclopedia of public administration, public policy and governance*. Cham: Springer International.

Garriga, E., & Melé, D. 2004. Corporate social responsibility theories: mapping the territory. *Journal of Business Ethics*, *53*(1), 51–71.

Hart, S.L. (2005). *Capitalism at the crossroads: the unlimited business opportunities in solving the world's most difficult problems*. Upper Saddle River, NJ: Pearson Education.

Hartman, L.P., & Werhane, P.H. (2013). Proposition: shared value as an incomplete mental model. *Business Ethics Journal Review*, *1*(6), 36–43.

Lantos, G.P. (2001). The boundaries of strategic corporate social responsibility. *Journal of Consumer Marketing*, *18*(7), 595–632.

Liczmańska-Kopcewicz, K., Mizera, K., & Pypłacz, P. (2019). Corporate social responsibility and sustainable development for creating value for FMCG sector enterprises. *Sustainability*, *11*(20), 5808.

Locke, R.M. (2003). The promise and perils of globalisation: the case of Nike. In T.A. Kochan and R. Schmalensee (Eds.), *Management: inventing and delivering its future*, pp. 39–70. Cambridge, MA: MIT Press.

McWilliams, A., & Siegel, D. (2001). Corporate social responsibility: a theory of the firm perspective. *Academy of Management Review*, *26*(1), 117–27.

McWilliams, A., & Siegel, D.S. (2011). Creating and capturing value: strategic corporate social responsibility, resource-based theory, and sustainable competitive advantage. *Journal of Management*, *37*(5), 1480–95.

Menghwar, P.S., & Daood, A. (2021). Creating shared value: a systematic review, synthesis and integrative perspective. *International Journal of Management Reviews*, *23*(4), 466–85.

Moon, H.C., & Parc, J. (2019). Shifting corporate social responsibility to corporate social opportunity through creating shared value. *Strategic Change*, *28*(2), 115–22.

Moon, H.C., Parc, J., Yim, S.H., & Park, N. (2011). An extension of Porter and Kramer's creating shared value (CSV): reorienting strategies and seeking international cooperation. *Journal of International and Area Studies*, *18*(2), 49–64.

Mühlbacher, H., & Böbel, I. (2019). From zero-sum to win-win – organisational conditions for successful shared value strategy implementation. *European Management Journal*, *37*(3), 313–24.

Nestlé (2011). Nestlé Creating Shared Value Report 2011. Retrieved from www.nestle.com/sites/default/files/asset-library/documents/library/documents/corporate_social_responsibility/2011-csv-report.pdf

Porter, M.E., & Kramer, M.R. (2002). The competitive advantage of corporate philanthropy. *Harvard Business Review*, *80*(12), 56–68.

Porter, M.E., & Kramer, M.R. (2006). Strategy and society: the link between competitive advantage and corporate social responsibility. *Harvard Business Review*, *84*(12), 78–92.

Porter, M.E., & Kramer, M.R. (2011). Creating Shared Value. *Harvard Business Review*, *89*(1), 62–77.

Porter, M.E., & Kramer, M.R. (2014). A response to Andrew Crane et al.'s article. *California Management Review*, *56*, 149–51.

Roszkowska-Menkes, M.T. (2018). Integrating strategic CSR and open innovation. Towards a conceptual framework. *Social Responsibility Journal*, *14*(4), 950–66.

Spitzeck, H., & Chapman, S. (2012). Creating shared value as a differentiation strategy – the example of BASF in Brazil. *Corporate*

Governance: *The International Journal of Business in Society, 12*(4), 499–513.

Von Liel, B. (2016). *Creating shared value as future factor of competition: analysis and empirical evidence.* Wiesbaden: Springer Nature.

Wójcik, P. (2016). How creating shared value differs from corporate social responsibility. *Journal of Management and Business Administration, 24*(2), 32–55.

3 A critical exegesis of the meaning of value

3.1 What essentially is value?

In the debate on Creating Shared Value (CSV), both sides are operating with a conception of economic value, which is seen as distinct from social or even moral value. We have already seen how CSV involves creating social and economic value for Porter and Kramer. 'CSV is integral to a company's profitability and competitive position. It leverages the unique resources and expertise of the company to create *economic value* by creating *social value* (italics is our emphasis)' (Porter & Kramer, 2011, p. 66). In the Crane et al. critique (2014) the same dichotomy is accepted: 'for roughly a century everybody in management academia took it for granted that business should not create any *value for society* at all … the only purpose of the firm has been to create *economic value* (italics is our emphasis)' (p. 142). While broadening the spectrum of authors who have taken positions in the debate, the situation does not change. For instance, de Los Reyes et al (2017, p. 143) affirm: 'we are able to highlight the strengths of CSV in "win-win" cases, where managers can identify an opportunity to create economic (one win) and *social value* (two wins) … (italics is our emphasis)'. Hartman and Werhane (2013, p. 37) declare to be in agreement 'to the concept that *economic value* is linked to *social value* rather than traditional philanthropy'. Although they also state that the current CSV approach of Porter and Kramer encourage the dichotomy – typical of Friedman – between business and society and point out that 'nor is it obvious that the concept of value can easily be parsed into "*economic*" and "*social*" categories, with traditional commerce concerned only with the former (italics is our emphasis)' (p. 38). However, in our

DOI: 10.4324/9781003398943-3

opinion, the conclusions come to not far-off from initial positions. In fact, they conclude their first criticism by arguing that

> there is much potential in the theory of shared value to erode this troubling dichotomy. In fact, by the structure of their own argument, they contend that the value (profit) created by the corporate practices they advocate shall be shared by businesses and the societies in which they operate. Accordingly, rather than limiting or moving beyond the original motive of profit maximisation (popularly, and often disparagingly, attributed to Friedman) it is specifically that motive that drives the shared value business model, which depicts simply a broader – shared – partnership between business and society toward a common goal of profitability, however defined.
>
> (p. 39)

It is clear that all of the participants in the debate accept this distinction of economic value from social value. In some sense, they accept a disjunction between business and society. Even those who dispute it do not want to understand why such a dichotomy cannot exist. In this study, we strongly want to assert that whatever one may think about how well business is serving society and/or social progress or about the power relations between companies and other prominent social actors, it is vital to remember that business is still an integral part of human society; it is indeed a social institution. In fact, beyond the individual entrepreneur's ends, any company is born with the function of putting in place the conditions through which human beings can satisfy their needs and desires, and consequently with the function of supporting the life existence conditions of the social system. It is, after all, an instrument of human action in the economic sphere (Ferrero, 1968). This function, which can well be defined as social – albeit mediated – is therefore intrinsic to any business enterprise. In 1967, Bartels (1967, p. 21) stated that 'business is primarily a social process, within which it is an economic process', in which the ethical standards generated by the society and the time in which the business is located, but also the expectations of the participants in the enterprise, need to be respected.

This truism (business as a social process/institution) leads us philosophically to question the dichotomy of economic value and social value. If the business is in society, then surely the 'economic value' created by the business must at least be part of 'social value'. This, in turn, leads us inexorably back to a fundamental question 'What essentially is value?' In general, if rational debate or even everyday discussion is to have the slightest hope of making any progress, there must be a high degree of convergence in the meaning of the terms used by the participants and, ideally, the identity of meaning (although such perfect identity of sense is difficult to achieve outside pure mathematics). So, in the case of the CSV debate, it is clearly essential to define '*value*' precisely. Nevertheless, while the participants do seem at least to have a high degree of convergence of sense in terms of economic value and social value, all participants are, we would argue, unfortunately, mistaken since once we recognise that business is in society and has a social function, this is an essentially false dichotomy.

We acknowledge that philosophically an in-depth elaboration on the meaning of 'value' or of any other fundamental concept can be carried out at three levels of analysis (Zanda et al., 2005):

- Ontological, if a value exists and what is it, which nature it has if it can be considered absolute or relative;
- Gnoseological, what methodology to use to identify, know, and appreciate value;
- Ethic-deontological: identifying norms underpinning the behaviour derived from this concept.

Focusing on an ontological level, it is necessary to recognise that the debate on the meaning of value is not new and passed through Greek philosophy, classical and neo-classical economics, as well as several branches of management studies, such as organisation studies, strategic management, and public management (Pitelis, 2009). Despite this, the value remains a particularly elusive term.

In Economics, the theory of value has played a central role, at least since Adam Smith. As Maurice Dobb shows in his 1973 classic *Theories of Value and Distribution since Adam Smith* (Dobb, 1973), for at least two centuries, economists have engaged in a rich and oscillating debate about the theory of value running through Adam Smith's cost of production theory, through the labour theory of value in Ricardo and Marx, to the subjectivist theories of marginal utility in Jevons and Menger. All of these theories will be noted are about the sources of relative values of goods and services (values in exchange) typically in a marketplace of some kind, and they assume that everyone knows what value in itself means. The debates on the theories of value in Economics, as outlined by Dobb and other historians of economic thought, are not about the meaning of value but about how value is generated. The only time when economists may have agonised a bit over the meaning of value in itself is when the classical economists considered the paradox of value (comparative values of diamonds and water) and were led to the distinction between value in use (later total utility) and value in exchange (later marginal utility). So, while economists have spent a great deal of time seeking to explain what gives rise to differences in relative values and how these are determined (supply/demand, labour theories of value, etc.), the precise (or we might say essential) meaning of 'value' in itself has been much less discussed. Joan Robinson (1964, p. 26) commented that

one of the great metaphysical ideas in Economics is expressed by the word 'value' ... it is not simply a price; it is something which will explain how prices come to be what they are. What is it? Where shall we find it? Like all metaphysical concepts when you try to pin it down it turns out to be just a word.

In Management thinking, it is taken as axiomatic that effective business is about the 'value proposition' (Oesterwalder, 2004); adding value in some sense is seen as the key to sustained competitive advantage (Porter, 1985) and, indeed, the essence of any business activity (Drucker, 2008). As in Economics, the term 'value' itself is rarely defined in this extensive literature, and not surprisingly, therefore, there have been subtle differences in how value and the 'value proposition' is interpreted, just as there have been differences among economists on what value means. Hence it would appear to be almost as much a metaphysical idea in Management theory as in Economics. However, here we seek to achieve something relatively less metaphysical and more elementary. We could even say pre-philosophical: to summarise the ways in which people have used and understood the terms 'value' and 'creation of value', especially in the literature of Economics and Management. In fact, we believe that a rigorous conceptual analysis of the term can provide a helpful prolegomenon to any discussion or controversy surrounding value in Economics and Management disciplines.

From an extremely basic logical view for the term value to be intelligible in everyday discourse (as it clearly is), there must be some elements of identity amid the various usages of the term. We would propose that if we look across all of the many uses of the term (economic value, social value, moral values or such simple statements as 'I value my free time') the identity lies in the *idea of enhancement of well-being*. An item or activity is valuable for a person or a society when it adds to their well-being, and so *the creation of value means making net additions to the well-being of at least some people*. We should emphasise that we are not trying to be prescriptive in this definition of value: we are simply proposing a conjecture based on the way the term has been used in everyday discourse by a wide variety of actors, both academic and lay, and this with a view to ensuring that we all understand each other in the debates surrounding value (or any other concept for that matter).[1]

At this point, however, we need to return to our initial starting point, i.e. the dichotomy between economic value and social value and our affirmation, i.e. that this dichotomy is false. This contrast is already emptied of meaning by defining value as an addition to well-being. Nevertheless, that is obviously not enough. In the following paragraphs, therefore, we intend to critically examine the economic and managerial thought on the concept of the value, understand how the dichotomy was created and what, if any, its foundations are.

3.2 The beginnings: the concept of value in Economics

Looking at Economics literature, the conception of value as a net addition to well-being has been central to the microeconomic theory of demand and consumer choice based on *marginal utility,* at least when well-being is interpreted in the narrow sense of the Utilitarian moral philosophers Jeremy Bentham (2007/1789) and John Stuart Mill (2018/1861). For Bentham, the utility was interpreted in a narrowly hedonistic sense as physical or at least material pleasure. With such a conception, it was easy enough to see how he was led to the idea of a 'felicific calculus of pleasure and pain'. Bentham could plausibly look forward to a time when we would be able to measure the net additions to pain or to pleasure by monitoring, for example, neuronal activity in the brain. Already with J.S. Mill's version of utilitarianism, however, the felicific calculus became less clear-cut because Mill included among the sources of utility purely spiritual or intellectual pleasures such as arise from reading a thought-provoking novel or philosophical work. While this may have meant that direct neuronal measurement of pleasure and pain was less plausible, economists in the twentieth century developed the technique of cost-benefit analysis intending to put monetary values on the pleasures and pains to arrive at an overall figure of net gain/diminution of pleasure generated in any activity or project in monetary terms (Eckstein, 1958; Mishan, 2021). In effect, the measurement is carried out in terms of people's willingness to pay for certain pleasures (or to avoid pains), and the willingness to pay principle can equally well be applied to physical as to spiritual or intellectual pleasures/pains. The estimation of willingness to pay is deduced either from market prices, where these exist and are pertinent, otherwise by surveys. These reflections, in turn, point to the fact that the notion of well-being could be interpreted in a wider sense than the purely utilitarian; for example, the Aristotelian conception of *eudaimonia* (roughly translatable as 'prospering'). Coming with such a broader conception and implicit in the Aristotelian approach is the suggestion that sometimes people may not be the best judges of what is ultimately for their own good/well-being, especially in the long term: for example, smoking as an ephemeral pleasure but with its long-term damaging health effects. With this development of the notion of well-being, cost-benefit analysis based on subjective measures of willingness to pay becomes problematic. Indeed, in recent decades the introduction of multi-criteria analysis that goes beyond traditional cost-benefit analysis, which is based in effect on the monetary estimation of marginal utilities in the appraisal of the welfare impact of public projects, recognises in effect that there can be more to well-being than simply the summation of net impacts on individual marginal utilities (e.g. Lindvall & Larsson, 2017; UK Government, 2009).

While marginalist explanations of the sources of value (or at least of value in exchange) today dominate microeconomic thinking on value, there have also been influential attempts to interpret value from what we might call the supply side in the labour theory of value and the various cost of production theories (Dobb, 1973). Nevertheless, to the extent that a good, service, or activity on which significant labour or other factor input is expended will have no value in any sense (market or otherwise) unless it is somehow enhancing the well-being of some person or group in society, the labour and cost of production theories implicitly presuppose the idea of the addition to well-being. To expend great efforts in producing goods nobody wants is just not a valuable activity in any sense: it is valueless. Certainly, Utilitarians are directly in line with our proposed conception of value since they would define it as morally valuable actions that add to some people's utility or subjective happiness (under the influence of Bentham's greatest happiness principle). It was in turn from the Utilitarians that economists developed and refined their conception of the value of goods and services in the work of the great nineteenth-century marginalists, Jevons, Menger, and Walras. In microeconomics, the value of a good or activity is identified with its marginal utility, the net addition to human happiness, which it makes possible (Stigler, 1972; Sloman & Wride, 2009). Alfred Marshall merged this marginalist conception with considerations of the impact of the supply side to arrive at the eventual market price of a good or service as determined by the interaction of supply (cost of production) and demand (marginal utility) (Marshall, 2013/1890). Keynes further endorsed the Marshallian conception in the preface to his *General Theory*, noting that 'our method of analysing the economic behaviour of the present under influence of changing ideas about the future is one which depends on the interaction of supply and demand, and is in this way linked up with our fundamental theory of value' (Keynes, 1936, p. xxii). This remains the centrepiece of the microeconomic theory of value to this day.

It should be emphasised that these various Utilitarians and economists were not only here fully in line with the basic definition we have offered (albeit with a utilitarian slant on the precise sense of well-being), they most certainly did not talk about 'economic value'; they simply spoke of value; that is to say value without any further qualification of the term. The only distinction we can find in pure microeconomic theory is between 'value-in-use' and 'value-in-exchange'. This has been proposed since the time of classical economics as the paradox of value: why have diamonds have such a high price and water such a low price when in terms of contribution to well-being, water is of primordial importance for survival, whereas one could easily live without diamonds. First of all, one notes the equivocation between price and value. However, the marginal utility theorists dissolved this paradox by making the mathematical distinction between the total utility offered by all of the units of a good service or activity consumed and the marginal utility, the extra utility derived from the last unit consumed. It is the latter which will be reflected in the price and not the former. Once this distinction is borne in mind and the relative abundance of water in relation to (market) demand is recognised, the paradox, which is in any case about relative prices and not total values, is dissolved. Thus the notion of value remains one in microeconomics and with the marginal utility, one is only mathematically distinguishing a total quantity and its rate of change as in mathematical physics' distinction between velocity and rate of change of velocity (acceleration). Therefore, the distinction between 'value in use' and 'value in exchange' is not somehow a distinction between two different concepts of value. Instead, to the extent that value is measurable in some sense because people can say that certain things are more valuable to them than others (even if only ordinal), then mathematically, there will be a number of facets of such measurement: total value, its first derivative (rate of change of value), second derivative, etc. But the essential concept of value remains the same throughout the various mathematical properties of its measurement.

3.3 The creation of the false dichotomy

3.3.1 The concept of value in Financial and Strategic Management

The assertion that economic value means profitability may seem harsh at first, but that is only because the identification is usually wrapped up in all manner of euphemisms. In this sense, Kay (1995, p. 19) defines '*value added*' *as* 'the difference between the value of the firm's ... output and the cost of the firm's (comprehensively accounted) inputs' and value added[2] is then seen as the 'key measure of corporate success'. The difference between the value of output and the value of the firm's inputs sounds suspiciously like profits to the present authors. In his *Strategic Management* textbook, the leading scholar Grant argues that long-term profit maximisation is a good proxy of a firm's value maximisation (2005, fifth edition). In their aforementioned work on strategic Corporate Social Responsibility (CSR), McWilliams and Siegel (2011, p. 1485) distinguish value for customers, value for society, and value for the firm; and they define the latter as 'the difference between revenue generated by resources used and the cost to the firm of the resources'. Probably the most uncompromising statement of this transition can be found in Jensen (2002) when in defending the idea that corporate managers be suitably focused and disciplined, he argues that there should be just one unambiguous and readily measurable objective for assessing managerial performance; and that that measurable objective should be in effect (long-run) profitability.

> Managers must have a criterion for deciding what is better and worse and better should be measured by the increase in the long term market value of the firm. I call this the Value Maximisation Proposition ... Briefly put value maximisation states that managers should make all decisions so as to increase the total long term market value of the firm. Total value is the sum of all financial claims on the firm including equity, debt, preferred stock and warrants.
>
> (Jensen, 2002, p. 236)

These are just some very explicit examples of an approach that has dominated much of the Strategic and Financial Management literature.

Moreover, according to Jensen, the maximisation of the company's value, thus understood, also leads to the most socially efficient solution; in other words, 'social value' is maximised when firms attempt to maximise their own total firm value (Jensen, 2002). The rootedness of this conception is also evident in – and was nurtured by – the words of Milton Friedman, who, in the 1970s, in response to the early emergence of CSR, stressed the subversive nature of the concept:

> This view [CSR] shows a fundamental misconception of the character and nature of a free economy. In such an economy, there is one and only one social responsibility of business – to use its resources and engage in activities designed to increase its

profits so long as it stays within the rules of the game, which is to say, engages in open and free competition, without deception or fraud.

(1962, ed. 2002, p. 133; see also Friedman, 1970)

It is interesting to reflect on how this evolution of the notion of value from the nineteenth-century marginalist utilitarian conception to the economic value as profitability of today's financial and strategic management literature has come about.

From the 1930s, economists and later Corporate Governance theorists became very exercised about the problems associated with the divorce of ownership (vested in shareholders) and control (managers, top executives) in contemporary large publicly quoted companies.[3] A line of theorising has been developed in this literature which has eventually come to be known as shareholder value (or shareholder wealth) maximisation theory. Managers should make decisions with the aim of maximising the 'value' of the firm, that is nothing more than its (stock) market valuation (Grossman & Stiglitz, 1977; Rappaport, 1986; Copeland et al., 1994; Jensen, 2002; Wallace, 2003). So to the extent that shareholder wealth depends directly on the share price and that profitability (in some sense)[4] determines share price, the creation of 'value' came to be identified with the creation of shareholder wealth, and so – again – profits. More generally, following this view, in Anglo-American common law corporate governance, the purpose of a company was deemed to be serving the interests of the owners, which in turn is interpreted as creating wealth for its owners, the shareholders. In this perspective, the equivalence 'value of the company = value for shareholders = profitability' is quite explicit. Countless other examples could be given from the literature as well as in practice. In a widely used Financial Management textbook (Petty, 2011, p. 8) it is stated right at the outset:

The goal of the firm is to maximise shareholder wealth. In effect this means maximising the market value of the existing shareholders' ordinary shares. We will see as this book unfolds that all financial decisions can be incorporated into this goal ... As we follow this goal throughout the book we must bear in mind that the shareholders are the legal owners of the firm.

The market value of shares of a specific company, while of course subject to the macroeconomic vagaries of bull and bear markets, is essentially dependent on investor expectations of future *profitability* of the company.

The Value-Based Management (VBM) approach and the consequent 'Economic Value Added' (EVA) measure are other examples of this confusion (Copeland et al., 1994; Young et al., 2000; Ittner & Larcker, 2001). VBM 'calls on managers to use value-based performance metrics for making better decisions' (Koller, 1994, p. 87). Among these metrics, it considers the residual income, i.e. the economic profit, as the best:

> Ideally, you should always set targets in terms of value, but since value is always based on long-term future cash flows and depends on an assessment of the future, short-term targets need a more immediate measure derived from actual performance over a single year. ... Economic profit measures the gap between what a company earns during a period and the minimum it must earn to satisfy its investors. Maximising economic profit over time will also maximise company value.
>
> (Koller, 1994, p. 98)

EVA is one of the most popular methods for calculating economic profit, and it is given by the difference between net operating profit after tax and cost of capital (Stewart, 1991; Ehrbar, 1998).

However, from the standpoint of a rigorous micro-economist, this tendency to identify value-added and so value creation with (any form of) profitability is a serious misconception; it involves a confusion of two manifestly separate ideas: that of value and that of profit. In addition, it must be emphasised that maximising value (understood as profitability) for shareholders, at least in the short term, does not necessarily coincide with maximising long-term value (understood as profitability) for the company. For instance, buyback strategies, i.e. reinvesting a large part of the profit in stock repurchases, are a typical example of money transfer from the company to the shareholders. The result is to reduce opportunities for job creation and investments in innovation and, ultimately, for the shareholders themselves, who will see their possible (future) earnings reduced (Lazonick, 2014; Block,

2018). Lazonick talks about a 'Downsize and Distribute' model (Lazonick & O'Sullivan, 2000).

3.3.2 A walk around a 'socially sensitive' stream: stakeholder theory and CSR literature

Although this perspective is still highly current, as evidenced in the textbooks mentioned above, since the late 1980s, the primacy of the shareholder value maximisation approach has been partly challenged, at least academically if not very much in practice, by stakeholder theory[5] (Freeman, 1984; Donaldson & Preston, 1995) and other constructs (i.e. CSR and its evolution) or managerial approaches, such as The Balanced Scorecard (Kaplan & Norton, 1992) and Triple Bottom Line (Elkington, 1997, 1998), which emphasise the need for measuring (and controlling) performance across multiple dimensions (e.g. social and environmental) and actors.

Abstracting from its relative specificities, this literature emphasises the need to modify objectives and tools for doing business in order to create economic, social, and environmental value.[6] Hence, this way, we seem to have arrived at the dichotomy between 'economic value' and 'social value'. We do not want to say here that the authors of these theories have all created the dichotomy directly. For example, if Kaplan (2009) speaks explicitly of economic, environmental, and social value, it does not seem that Freeman did the same in elaborating and defending the stakeholder theory.[7] Instead, we want to assert that these theories have laid the foundations for this dichotomy has been created and then entrenched by future developments in literature.

For stakeholder theory, a company exists to benefit not just its shareholders but all those 'who can affect or are affected by' the company's activities (Freeman, 1984, p. 46), e.g. employees, customers, suppliers, and the local community. From this point of view, the continuity and success of a company also depend on its stakeholders and the relationship that it can establish with them. Hence, the task of top management is to manage and shape these relationships in order to create greater value for all stakeholders, including the shareholders. However, the theory does not clarify in any concrete way what 'all stakeholders value maximisation' really means, or, at least, it does not solve that question. Indeed, that ambiguity and the fact that it left managers free to make their own preferred trade-offs between different stakeholder interests was the main reason for Jensen's opposition to the stakeholder approach (Jensen, 2002).

Parmar et al. (2010) and Freeman et al. (2010), in fact, highlighted that the questions related to the creation and trade of value, what precisely 'value' means for a particular group of stakeholders, how firms can create these different types of 'value' for stakeholders and how they can be measured are still open. Phillips et al. (2003, p. 486) argue that

> maximising value says nothing about who gets a say in the decision-making or who gets how much of this value, so maximised. It is only when the primary beneficiary of this profitability is constantly and exclusively a single stakeholder (e.g., equity share owners) that there is conflict between the theories. An organisation that is managed for stakeholders will distribute the fruits of organisational success (and failure) among all legitimate stakeholders.

Here, we can clearly see that even in the stakeholder theory, the equivalence between value and profitability persists or, at least, it is not excluded. What mainly changes are the distribution of these profits and the participation in the decision-making process. On this point, more recently, Freeman and colleagues (2020) have made what we would call a step forward from the starting position. While asserting the existence of multiple types of value (which, as we have said, we dispute), the leading authors of stakeholder theory explicitly reject the equation value = profit by arguing that the total value created is a function of the total value created for all stakeholders. However, they also admit that there is a need to investigate further what value means.

Also, when looking at CSR literature, the effective dominance of profitability/shareholder wealth maximisation as the ultimate goal of business strategy may appear in the guise of the 'business case for CSR'. There is extensive literature seeking to examine the correlation or otherwise of CSR activities with firm financial performance and profitability (Cho et al., 2019; Aupperle et al., 1985, to cite but two examples early and late of a vast literature);

and there have been repeated attempts to show that ultimately
engaging in CSR activities (broadly defined) can contribute to a
firm's profitability and that therefore there is a clear 'business case'
for pursuing such CSR (and of course not so often emphasised,
for avoiding CSR activities which do not contribute to a firm's
ultimate bottom line profitability).[8] As Carroll and Shabana argue,

> the business case for CSR refers to the arguments that provide
> rational justification for CSR initiatives from a primarily cor-
> porate economic/financial perspective. Business case arguments
> contend that firms which engage in CSR activities will be
> rewarded by the market in economic and financial terms.
> (Carroll & Shabana, 2010, p. 101)

The critical point about the business case approach is that corporate strategy and managerial decision-making are still entirely
subservient to the ultimate profit-making goal, as outlined by
Friedman and Jensen in their various ways. CSR activities are not
something which derives in any way from a sense of 'moral values'
but rather selected ethical-looking activities which contribute to
firms' financial performance to 'economic value' as measured
ultimately by profitability. It should be emphasised that when
Porter and Kramer seek to reconcile, through their approach,
the pursuit of profitability as a guarantee of economic sustainability of the company with the contribution to social progress is
certainly not a rehash of the business case approach as outlined
above. In fact, they want companies to contribute, as they put it, to
'economic value' as well as to 'social value', even if the social value
remains somewhat vaguely defined as a company's 'contribution to
social progress' to 'advancing the economic and social conditions
in the communities in which it operates' (Porter & Kramer, 2011,
p. 67).

Moreover, it would be simplistic to say that the CSR literature can
be reduced to the business case, and this is certainly different from
what we want to do. As mentioned in Chapter 2, CSR is a moving
target, and alongside the 'instrumental' theories, there are ethical,
political, and integrative ones (Garriga & Melè, 2004). However,
some authors emphasise how these differences are, in part, evolutionary and how CSR moves from the initial ethical/normative
approach to the instrumental one (Lee, 2008). Obviously, many of

these distinctions exist in scientific debate and less so in practice. In their article 'Focusing on Value: Reconciling Corporate Social Responsibility, Sustainability and a Stakeholder: Approach in a Network World', Wheeler and others (2003) proposed a (descriptive) framework of organisational culture, characterised by three levels, i.e. avoiding the destruction of value (economic, social or ecological), value neutrality or trade-offs, maximising value (economic, social or ecological), also arguing that the tensions between normative/ethical and instrumental approaches are of little use to practice. Some years later, Carroll wrote:

> CSR has never been pure altruism, although some idealists would like it to be the driving motivation. In fact, businesses engage in CSR because they see in the framework the benefits for them as well as society. This is enlightened self-interest that has come of age, and there is no going back.
>
> (Carroll, 2015, p. 95)

From this excursus, we seem to have, on the one hand, found the start of the 'false dichotomy' (economic vs social), and on the other hand, to have reaffirmed the tendency in the literature (1) to confuse economic value with profit, leaving the concept of social value unclear or (2) to avoid defining the concept of value itself.

Nonetheless, one can find some definitions closer to ours within the managerial literature. Harrison and Wicks (2013, pp. 100–1) 'define "value" broadly as anything that has the potential to be of worth to stakeholders'. Similarly, in an interesting study aimed at proposing a framework to explore the nature, determinants, trade-offs, causal pathways, co-evolution and co-determination between value capture and value creation, Pitelis (2009) first pointed – and we are in agreement, as mentioned above – that both the economic and managerial literature focuses on compound concepts (such as added value or value capture/creation), but often fails to define value per se. He then suggests defining value at the level of the individual economic agent at any rate as 'perceived worthiness of a subject matter to a socio-economic agent that is exposed to and/or can make use of the subject matter in question' (Pitelis, 2009, p. 1118). These definitions are certainly going in the same direction as our proposed definition in terms of the net addition to well-being, but there is, we believe, an equivocation inherent in the term 'worthiness' (what makes a subject matter worthy? addition to well-being perhaps?). These usages of the term value, while readily applicable to economic and management theory, would be difficult to extend to moral values without circularity of definition.

Furthermore, several interesting perspectives come from the literature regarding service management, within which some of the authors reflect fleetingly on the meaning of value itself and there is a certain convergence with the notion we have proposed of value as a net addition to well-being. For example, Vargo and colleagues (Vargo et al., 2008, p. 149) have proposed that one 'define value simply in terms of an improvement of system well-being' where the system refers to a service system or service network. However, in this and other works, Vargo and his co-authors seem to retain the distinction of value-in-use and value-in-exchange as somehow two different concepts of value (we already showed in a previous paragraph that they represent only two different measurements). According to their view, it is value-in-use that is, thus, defined as 'improvement on system well-being'. This persistence with two separate ideas or sorts of value can also be bound in a later work of Vargo et al. (2017), where they assert:

> Although business disciplines generally continue to centre on value-in-exchange as a primary measure of value, the marketing discipline has shifted over time to consider other value related concepts such as customer satisfaction … these customer-centric views draw attention to the need to study value-in-use because they are based on the assessment of value through customer-firm interaction or the use of a market offering.
>
> (Vargo et al., 2017, p. 118)

3.4 Value creation vs value capture: the distributional question

It will, we hope, be evident from the above exposition that the notion of 'economic value' identified with shareholder wealth maximisation involves a somewhat different usage of the term from the fundamental meaning of value as marginal utility (or net contribution to well-being) that we find in basic marginalist microeconomics or from a wider notion of value as a net contribution to well-being in society as a whole such as we are proposing. The marginal utility is not in any way profit; at best, we might identify profitability loosely with Marx's 'creation of surplus value'. Karl Marx argued that in capitalist economies, there could be a creation of 'surplus value' as goods and services are transformed by human labour power in a manner which creates extra value on the basic raw materials and labour time used.[9] This surplus value is the source of profitability of a business (Marx, 1969/1905–1910). If we wish to be precise, surplus value is not identical to profit since, strictly speaking, it represents the surplus over and above raw materials cost *plus* the subsistence wage cost of the labour employed, but it remains the ultimate source of profit for the capitalist owners.

Alternatively, one might protest that profits create marginal utility for shareholders. Nevertheless, that immediately raises the distributional question (to which further reference will be made below) of why so much focus is just on the value created for shareholders; and the even more fundamental question of whether receiving more dividends or capital gains actually increases a wealth-holder's utility/well-being. There may be more to the good life than making ever more money. So profit, in short, is not value per se, nor indeed is it some kind of strange beast called 'economic value' or 'shareholder value'. As an annual economic income, the determined profit is a conventional economic quantity, unlike the value created, i.e. a real magnitude, the result of the enterprise's production, even more intricate and complex to measure. It is no coincidence that in the literature, we talk about annual operating income as an economic quantity attributed[10] to a period and not calculated (Onida, 1960). This is why the annual income of the enterprise, as a result of evaluations and estimates, often arbitrary, is considered a conjectured economic quantity, that is, abstract. Accounting standards can be seen as the tools to contain an inevitable arbitrariness, although it must be stressed that this levee is sometimes moved or broken, as in the case of creative accounting or fraud (Jones, 2011).

Case example 3.1 The profit as a conjectured and conventionally measured part of the value

Asea Brown Boveri (ABB) is a Swiss-Swedish multinational working in the robotics, energy, and automation markets. It has a long and illustrious history of technological leadership and innovation. During the 1990s, ABB won several business honours and was held up as a standard for management practice worldwide. In 1999–2001, it was ranked number one in its market sector – Industrial Goods and Services – in corporate sustainability by the Dow Jones Sustainability Index (DJSI). In February 2000, its market value was approximately € 47,300 million, exceeding every best expectation of its shareholders. However, the analysts had not considered that the automation market was struggling. In addition, ABB was carrying out an acquisition strategy, which failed to compensate for the divestments. The second quarter did, therefore, record a poor result. In the same year, to be able to list on the US stock exchange (the listing took place in 2001), it switched from International Accounting Standard (IAS) to Generally Accepted Accounting Principles (GAAP). At the time, there were several significant differences between the two sets of principles. As a result of this change, 40% of the reported net income for 2000 'vanished' due to different accounting treatments of non-operating income with the gains from the sales of these various assets. Under IAS, counting the gains from selling these multiple assets in one's operating income was possible. This accounting practice was not permitted under GAAP. At the beginning of 2022, ABB reported a US$ 691 million net loss for 2001, the first loss in the company's history since 1934.

Source: Adaptation from Jones M. (Ed.) (2011). *Creative accounting, fraud and international accounting scandals*, Wiley, New York, pp. 365–8.

With that conceptual confusion regarding supposedly different types of value cleared out of the way, we may wonder if there is any indirect linkage between profits and value. Well, actually, Porter's own earlier work on value creation in the supply chain and the five forces determining competitiveness (Porter, 1980, 1985) provide the linkage. A business which creates lots of value (marginal utility) for people in a society will (at least under conditions of competition in the marketplace) be able to make greater profits than one which creates less value (marginal utility). However, the profits are the *fruits or resultant* of successful value creation in a capitalist system; they are the surplus which, under the distributional set-up of capitalism, accrue to the firm's owners but could be distributed in alternative ways. It is a ghastly but all too common and simplistic mistake to identify the creation of value with what is a mere by-product of such value creation in a capitalist system: profits distributed to shareholders. At best, the latter is not about value creation but rather about *value capture*;[11] that is to say, about the essentially distributional question of who gains financially from the value that has been co-created in business organisations. But while profitable business can arise from successful value creation and capture of that value for shareholders, it is by no means true that all profitable businesses represent value creation, thus underlining that profitability and value must not be elided or confused. To drive this point home, consider the following three examples: a company which is engaging in some kind of total scam (selling non-existent products on the Internet, for example, and unfortunately it does happen quite a lot today) may be highly profitable, but we could hardly consider it to be creating value. It is simple theft or, more euphemistically, wealth transfer without any net value creation. Or consider a Ponzi scheme such as Bernie Madoff's;[12] very profitable for Bernie, but no value was being created (Berman & Knight, 2009). Or consider, on the other hand, a state-owned enterprise which may be operated at some kind of break-even level whereby it reinvests all of its surplus in new equipment etc. No profits per se are being generated, and there are no shareholders to serve (apart from the State), but value (increases in well-being/utility) can certainly be created for many people in society by such enterprises.

Case example 3.2 Does profit always create value?

Nike is the world leader in sporting goods. It is one of the best-known brands worldwide, and many stars have worn its sneakers. Among the top 10 most expensive Nike shoe endorsements are Michael Jordan, Tiger Woods, Rafael Nadal, Roger Federer, and Kobe Bryant. Despite this, Nike has been at the centre of numerous scandals that have compromised its image, and it took years to clean up its act.

The company was booming between 1971 (i.e. foundation year) and the early 1990s. It became the world's largest seller of athletic footwear in a few years. In 1995, its net income after tax was $ 399,664, more than 38 times that of 1985. Hand in hand with success, accusations from activists about sweatshops and child labour in its Asian factories arose and grew in the 1990s.

For many years, Nike has denied these allegations, but the protests of activists (not only NGOs but also consumers who no longer buy) have not stopped. In 2005 Nike published a 108-page report providing information on 700 factories that produced its footwear and clothing and acknowledging the validity of the accusations, particularly regarding the Asian factories. Among the abusive treatments admitted by the company were low wages, lack of one day off a week, forced overtime, and limited access to toilets and drinking water during the working day.

Sources: https://financesonline.com/top-10-most-expensive-nike-shoes-endorsements-from-kobe-bryant-to-tiger-woods/; www.theguardian.com/business/2005/apr/14/ethicalbusiness.money; Spar, D.L., & La Mure, L.T. (2003). The power of activism: assessing the impact of NGOs on global business. *California Management Review*, *45*(3), 78–101.

The issue is prominent even if observed from a pure accounting perspective, in which the difference between value and profit is enhanced. In fact, in order to enable the distribution to shareholders of a profit, whatever it is and at any cost, international and generally accepted accounting standards (i.e. IFRS; GAAP) promote a profit configuration obtained through 'fair value', paying little attention to distributional issues (Anthony et al., 2011; Nobes & Robert, 2020). It should be noted that the same issue could be addressed through more prudent or neutral accounting principles (Jones, 2011). So, the obstinate search for a profit to distribute to shareholders has made us lose sight of the concept of value for the company and society as a whole.

The aforementioned buyback strategy is another useful example. We notice that this approach has disadvantaged companies, less inclined to investments and long-term results, and the economic system needs to be more productive and prosperous (Lazonick, 2014; Block, 2018).

This difference is also evident in the case of companies in crisis, which, while not generating profit, can continue to create value (for example, by continuing to operate in an area where it would be difficult for workers to reallocate in the job market).

In the end, therefore, profitability cannot be identified with the creation of value. It has, at most, a link with value capture; it has to do with the question of distribution of the rewards which may accrue to a productive enterprise from the successful creation of value in a market economy or, as Marx would have said, about the distribution of the 'surplus value'. In American-style capitalism, that reward or 'dividend' is paid to the shareholders; in a state-owned enterprise, it is reinvested (or accrues to the government), while in a cooperative enterprise, it is distributed among the entire workforce (who, in effect, are all shareholders). It will be noted that our purpose here is not in any way to take sides in ideological debates about optimal socio-economic business models, fascinating as they may be; it is simply to show that profitability is not about the creation of some kind of special 'economic value'; rather it is a by-product reward and just one possible way in which the reward from value creation in a market system may be distributed; and, we should emphasise, not every profitable business creates value as lucrative criminal activities and corruption amply testify.

Notes

1 As much as certain spin doctors and media manipulators may like to pretend otherwise to serve their propaganda purposes, we are not actually in Alice in Wonderland, where everyone chooses the meaning of the words they use. There are grim realities that cannot just be spun or wished away. Or perhaps we are in Alice's Wonderland and communication has broken down completely between certain human groups.

2 In truth, the concept of Added Value and its distribution has been more recently also deepened in a social or sustainability key to better highlight how all the subjects and stakeholders who participate in creating wealth should be remunerated. See, for instance, Perera Aldama, L., & Zicari, A. (2012). Value-added reporting as a tool for sustainability: a Latin American experience. *Corporate Governance: The International Journal of Business in Society*, *12*(4), 485–98; De Chernatony, L.,

Harris, F., & Dall'Olmo Riley, F. (2000). Added value: its nature, roles and sustainability. *European Journal of Marketing*, *34*(1/2), 39–56.

3 While not going into detail here, it is interesting to remember that the doctrine identifies various historical phases in the economic system, each characterised by a specific form of legitimation of the power of government in the corporate system, given by the possession of the scarcest production factor (phase of ownership of land, capital ownership phase, managerial capitalism phase, equity-financial managerial capitalism phase). On this point, see also Zanda G. (2009). *Il governo della grande impresa nella società della conoscenza*. Torino: Giappichelli.

4 We say in some sense because, of course, there is a whole debate about short-term vs long-term profitability and about which is the aim of contemporary shareholders. That debate need not concern us here since the key point is that share price reflects some kind of profitability.

5 In truth, we have already mentioned Bartels, who, already in 1967, spoke of the legitimate expectations of the participants in the company.

6 On the issue, a paper by Donaldson is of great interest with his epistemological framework for understanding value creation. A valuable tool for scholars of the relationship between value and the way of doing business for Donaldson would be precisely the relationship between ideas and actions: 'The key to the practical inference approach that I offer here consists in two connected concepts: intrinsic values and practical reasoning' (p. 3). Donaldson, T. (2021). Values ground value creation: the practical inference framework. *Organization Theory*, *2*, 1–27. DOI: 10.1177/26317877211036712.

7 However, it should be emphasised that this dichotomy is not entirely extraneous to the author, especially in more recent works. For instance, in Freeman, R.E., Phillips, R., & Sisodia, R. (2020). Tensions in stakeholder theory. *Business & Society*, *59*(2), 213–31, he and his colleagues argue 'Every business has always created and sometimes destroyed multiple kinds of value (e.g., financial, intellectual, social, emotional, spiritual, cultural, and ecological) for customers, suppliers, employees, communities, and financiers' (p. 225) or 'It is not stakeholders versus shareholders, or economic versus social value. In today's business world, "and" is the most important word' (p. 226).

8 Considerable doubts have emerged not only on CSR or sustainability practices but also, and one could say consequently, on related reporting practices as well. Disclosure would therefore be a tool to create a gap between the talk and the walk, i.e. a tool of hypocrisy and organisational facades through which managing stakeholders' expectations and interests. On this issue, see, for instance, Cho, C.H., Laine, M., Roberts, R.W., & Rodrigue, M. (2015). Organised hypocrisy, organisational façades, and sustainability reporting. *Accounting, Organisations and Society*, *40*, 78–94; Higgins, C., Tang, S., & Stubbs, W. (2020).

On managing hypocrisy: the transparency of sustainability reports. *Journal of Business Research, 114*, 395–407.

9   It is also helpful to remember the relationship between time and value, which has been explored under many aspects in the social sciences and which was recalled by Marx himself. Interesting readings on the topic are Cohen, E.F. (2018). *The political value of time: citizenship, duration, and democratic justice.* Cambridge: Cambridge University Press; Jessop, B. (2002). Time and space in the globalisation of capital and their implications for state power. *Rethinking Marxism, 14*(1), 97–117.

10   In this regard, it is emphasised that the need for this periodic 'attribution' does not derive only from the desire to distribute dividends or the opportunity to equalise incomes between several financial years but also from purely fiscal duties, i.e. paying taxes.

11   Speaking of capture, it cannot be waived here to also refer to State Capture, understood as a form of prevarication of the interests of companies aimed at guaranteeing profits and earnings that would otherwise not be realisable. By illegally contributing to the formation of laws, private power groups capture the State by means of corruption and pressure, weakening its functions. This generates profits and economic results to the detriment of other companies and the collective well-being (Hellman, J.S., Geraint, J., & Kaufmann, D. (2000). *Seize the state, seize the day: state capture, corruption and influence in transition.* World Bank Working Paper 2444. Washington, DC: The World Bank). Basically, part of the value produced by companies is the result of behaviours that tend to capture the State. On this point, it is interesting to understand how crony capitalism has, in fact, transformed entire entrepreneurial elites and their culture of value (The new age of crony capitalism, *The Economist*, 13 March 2014).

12   Bernie Madoff, for many years, ran one of the biggest Ponzi schemes ever known but was exposed for the fraud he was in 2009. There are various detailed press accounts of his scheme in all of the financial and general newspapers at the time. In particular, we may make reference to Berman and Knight (2009). What did Bernard Madoff do? *Harvard Business Review*, 30 June 2009.

References

Anthony, R.N., Hawkins, D.F., Merchant, K.A., Wang, L., & Du, M. (2011). *Accounting: text and cases* (13th ed.). New York: Irwin/McGraw-Hill.

Aupperle, K.E., Carroll, A.B., & Hatfield, J.D. (1985). An empirical examination of the relationship between corporate social responsibility and profitability. *Academy of Management Journal, 28*(2), 446–63.

Bartels, R. (1967). A model for ethics in marketing. *Journal of Marketing*, *31*(1), 20–6.

Bentham, J. (2007). *An introduction to the principles of morals and legislation*. Dover Philosophical Classics. New York: Dover Publications. (Original work first published in 1789.)

Berman, K., & Knight, J. (2009). What did Bernard Madoff do? *Harvard Business Review*, 30 June 2009.

Block, F.L. (2018). *Capitalism. The future of an illusion*. Oakland, CA: University of California Press.

Carroll, A.B. (2015). Corporate social responsibility: the centerpiece of competing and complementary frameworks. *Organizational Dynamics*, *44*(2), 87–96.

Carroll, A.B., & Shabana, K.M. (2010). The business case for corporate social responsibility: a review of concepts, research and practice. *International Journal of Management Reviews*, *12*(1), 85–105.

Cho, C.H., Laine, M., Roberts, R.W., & Rodrigue, M. (2015). Organized hypocrisy, organizational façades, and sustainability reporting. *Accounting, Organizations and Society*, *40*, 78–94.

Cho, S.J., Chung, C.Y., & Young, J. (2019). Study on the relationship between CSR and financial performance. *Sustainability*, *11*(2), 343.

Cohen, E.F. (2018). *The political value of time: citizenship, duration, and democratic justice*. Cambridge: Cambridge University Press.

Copeland, T., Koller, T., & Murrin, J. (1994). *Valuation: managing and measuring the value of companies*. New York: Wiley.

Crane, A., Palazzo, G., Spence, L.J., & Matten, D. (2014). Contesting the value of 'creating shared value'. *California Management Review*, *56*(2), 130–53.

De Chernatony, L., Harris, F., & Dall'Olmo Riley, F. (2000). Added value: its nature, roles and sustainability. *European Journal of Marketing*, *34*(1/2), 39–56.

de los Reyes Jr, G., Scholz, M., & Smith, N.C. (2017). Beyond the 'win-win' creating shared value requires ethical frameworks. *California Management Review*, *59*(2), 142–67.

Dobb, M. (1973). *Theories of value and distribution since Adam Smith: ideology and economic theory*. Cambridge: Cambridge University Press.

Donaldson, T. (2021). Values ground value creation: the practical inference framework. *Organization Theory*, *2*, 1–27. DOI: 10.1177/26317877211036712.

Donaldson, T., & Preston, L.E. (1995). The stakeholder theory of the corporation: concepts, evidence and implications. *Academy of Management Review*, *20*(1), 65–91.

Drucker, P. (2008). *The essential Drucker*. New York: Harper Collins.

Eckstein, O. (1958). *Water resource development: the economics of project evaluation.* Cambridge, MA: Harvard University Press.

Ehrbar, A. (1998). *EVA: the real key to creating wealth.* New York: Wiley.

Elkington, J. (1997). *Cannibals with forks: the triple bottom line of 21st century business.* Stony Creek, CT: New Society Publishers.

Elkington, J. (1998). Partnerships from cannibals with forks: the triple bottom line of 21st-century business. *Environmental Quality Management*, 8(1), 37–51.

Ferrero, G. (1968). *Istituzioni di economia d'azienda.* Milan: Giuffrè.

Freeman, R.E. (1984). *Strategic management: a stakeholder perspective.* Boston, MA: Pitman.

Freeman, R.E., Harrison, J.S., Wicks, A.C., Parmar, B.L., & De Colle, S. (2010). *Stakeholder theory: the state of the art.* Cambridge: Cambridge University Press.

Freeman, R.E., Phillips, R., & Sisodia, R. (2020). Tensions in stakeholder theory. *Business & Society*, 59(2), 213–31.

Friedman, M. (1962, edition 2002). *Capitalism and freedom.* Chicago, IL: Chicago University Press.

Friedman, M. (1970). The social responsibility of business is to increase profits. *New York Times Magazine*, 13 December. Retrieved from www.nytimes.com/1970/09/13/archives/a-friedman-doctrine-the-social-responsibility-of-business-is-to.html

Garriga, E., & Melé, D. (2004). Corporate social responsibility theories: mapping the territory. *Journal of Business Ethics*, 53(1), 51–71.

Grant, R.M. (2005). *Contemporary strategy analysis.* Hoboken, NJ: Blackwell Publishing.

Grossman, S.J., & Stiglitz, J.E. (1977). On value maximization and alternative objectives of the firm. *Journal of Finance*, 32(2), 389–402.

Harrison, J.S., & Wicks, A.C. (2013). Stakeholder theory, value, and firm performance. *Business Ethics Quarterly*, 23(1), 97–124.

Hartman, L.P., & Werhane, P.H. (2013). Proposition: shared value as an incomplete mental model. *Business Ethics Journal Review*, 1(6), 36–43.

Hellman, J.S., Geraint, J., & Kaufmann, D. (2000). *Seize the state, seize the day: state capture, corruption and influence in transition.* World Bank Working Paper 2444. Washington, DC: The World Bank.

Higgins, C., Tang, S., & Stubbs, W. (2020). On managing hypocrisy: the transparency of sustainability reports. *Journal of Business Research*, 114, 395–407.

Ittner, C.D., & Larcker, D.F. (2001). Assessing empirical research in managerial accounting: a value-based management perspective. *Journal of Accounting and Economics*, 32(1–3), 349–410.

Jensen, M.C. (2002). Value maximization, stakeholder theory, and the corporate objective function. *Business Ethics Quarterly*, 12(2), 235–56.

Jessop, B. (2002). Time and space in the globalisation of capital and their implications for state power. *Rethinking Marxism, 14*(1), 97–117.

Jones, M. (Ed.) (2011). *Creative accounting, fraud and international accounting scandals.* New York: Wiley.

Kaplan, R.S. (2009). Conceptual foundations of the balanced scorecard. *Handbooks of Management Accounting Research, 3*, 1253–69.

Kaplan, R.S., & Norton, D.P. (1992). The balanced scorecard: measures that drive performance. *Harvard Business Review, 70*(1), 71–9.

Kay, J. (1995). *Foundations of corporate success: how business strategies add value.* Oxford: Oxford University Press.

Keynes, J.M. (1936). *General theory of employment interest and money.* London: Macmillan.

Koller, T. (1994). What is value-based management? *McKinsey Quarterly, 3*, 87–101.

Lazonick, W. (2014). Profits without prosperity. *Harvard Business Review, 92*(9), 46–55.

Lazonick, W., & O'Sullivan, M. (2000). Maximizing shareholder value: a new ideology for corporate governance. *Economy and Society, 29*(1), 13–35.

Lee, M.D.P. (2008). A review of the theories of corporate social responsibility: its evolutionary path and the road ahead. *International Journal of Management Reviews, 10*(1), 53–73.

Lindvall, N., & Larsson, A. (2017). Investment Appraisal in the public sector: incorporating Flexibility and Environmental Impact. *Journal of Advanced Management Studies, 5*(3), 182–9.

Marshall, A. (2013). *Principles of economics.* Palgrave Macmillan Classic. London: Macmillan. (Original work first published in 1890.)

Marx, K. (1969). *Theories of surplus value. The capital, Vol. IV.* London: Lawrence & Wishart. (Original work published 1905–1910.)

McWilliams, A., & Siegel, D.S. (2011). Creating and capturing value: strategic corporate social responsibility, resource-based theory, and sustainable competitive advantage. *Journal of Management, 37*(5), 1480–95.

Mill, J.S. (2018). *Utilitarianism.* Bishop Auckland: Aziloth Books. (Original work first published in 1861.)

Mishan, E. (2021) *Cost benefit analysis* (6th ed.). London: Routledge.

Nobes, C., & Parker, R.B. (2020). *Comparative international accounting* (14th ed.). Upper Saddle River, NJ: Pearson Education.

Oesterwalder, A. (2004). *Business model ontology.* Retrieved from www. hec.unil.ch/aosterwa/PhD/Osterwalder_PhD_BM_Ontology.pdf, accessed 2 April 2021.

Onida, P. (1960). *Economia d'azienda.* Trattato italiano di economia, vol. 9. Turin: Unione tipografico-editrice torinese.

Parmar, B.L., Freeman, R.E., Harrison, J.S., Wicks, A.C., Purnell, L., & De Colle, S. (2010). Stakeholder theory: the state of the art. *Academy of Management Annals, 4*(1), 403–45.

Perera Aldama, L. & Zicari, A. (2012). Value-added reporting as a tool for sustainability: a Latin American experience. *Corporate Governance: The International Journal of Business in Society, 12*(4), 485–98.

Petty, J.W. (2011). *Financial management: principles and applications* (6th ed.). Frenchs Forest, NSW: Pearson Australia.

Phillips, R., Freeman, R.E., & Wicks, A.C. (2003). What stakeholder theory is not. *Business Ethics Quarterly, 13*(4), 479–502.

Pitelis, C.N. (2009). The co-evolution of organizational value capture, value creation and sustainable advantage. *Organization Studies, 30*(10), 1115–39.

Porter, M.E. (1980). *Competitive strategy.* New York: Free Press.

Porter, M.E. (1985). *Competitive advantage: creating and sustaining superior performance.* New York: Free Press.

Porter, M.E., & Kramer, M. (2011). Creating Shared Value. *Harvard Business Review, 89*(1), 62–77.

Rappaport, A. (1986). *Creating shareholder value: a guide for managers & investors.* New York: Free Press.

Robinson, J. (1964). *Economic philosophy.* Harmondsworth: Pelican Books.

Sloman, J., & Wride, A. (2009). *Economics* (7th ed.). Harlow: Pearson Prentice Hall.

Spar, D.L., & La Mure, L.T. (2003). The power of activism: assessing the impact of NGOs on global business. *California Management Review, 45*(3), 78–101.

Stewart, G.B. (1991). *The quest for value.* New York: Harper Collins.

Stigler, G.J. (1972). The adoption of Marginal Utility Theory. *History of Political Economy, 4*(2), 571–86.

UK Government. (2009). *Multi-criteria analysis: a manual.* Retrieved online from https://assets.publishing.service.gov.uk/government/uploads/system/uploads/attachment_data/file/7612/1132618.pdf, accessed 23 February 2023.

Vargo, S.L., Akaka, M.A., & Vaughan, C.M. (2017). Conceptualizing value: a service-ecosystem view. *Journal of Creating Value, 3*(2), 117–24.

Vargo, S.L., Maglio, P.P., & Akaka, M.A. (2008). On value and value co-creation: a service systems and service logic perspective. *European Management Journal, 26*(3), 145–52.

Wallace, J.S. (2003). Value maximization & stakeholder theory: compatible or not? *Journal of Applied Corporate Finance, 15*(3), 120–7.

Wheeler, D., Colbert, B., & Freeman, R.E. (2003). Focusing on value: reconciling corporate social responsibility, sustainability and a stakeholder approach in a network world. *Journal of General Management, 28*(3), 1–28.

Young, S.D., O'Byrne, S.F., Young, D.S., & Young, S. (2000). *EVA and value-based management*. New York: McGraw-Hill Professional Publishing.

Zanda, G. (2009). *Il governo della grande impresa nella società della conoscenza*. Turin: Giappichelli Editore.

Zanda, G., Lacchini, M., & Onesti, T. (2005). *La valutazione delle aziende*. Turin: Giappichelli Editore.

4 The disputed naivety of Creating Shared Value and its roots in a primordial contrast

4.1 A naive or rather an optimist concept?

In the previous chapter, we argued that what lies behind the terminology of 'economic value', as used by all participants in the debate, is the idea of shareholder wealth generation and, thus, in effect, of profits for this one (privileged because of ownership) stakeholder group, i.e. an essentially *distributional* question. Intertwined theorising about value and distribution is widely present in the long history of economic thought, and indeed given the implicit ideological tinting of the way economists invariably approach their theoretical work, that value and distribution should be so connected is perhaps inevitable (Dobb, 1973; Myrdal, 1959) even if not always analytically helpful. In Management and Organisational theory, there is a similar intertwining and tension between value creation and value capture (Brandenburger & Harborne, 1996; Pitelis, 2009). Under the influence of these tensions, the debate on Creating Shared Value (CSV) has centred on the question of whether 'economic value' creation is compatible with 'social value' creation. But, in our opinion, this involves a serious misunderstanding by both sides in the discussion since there is only one value (net additions to human well-being); the economic value vs social value dichotomy is not, therefore, about value creation but about *value capture*: about the *distribution* of the spoils from value creation.

With the notion of value and its distinction from profitability thus clarified, it will be interesting to return to the CSV debate with which we began our reflections. As seen, the criticisms of the notion of CSV put forward by Crane et al. (2014), and other opponents, suggest that CSV ignores the tensions between

DOI: 10.4324/9781003398943-4

economic and social goals and is naive about business compliance. Essentially, Crane et al. (2014) suggest that Porter and Kramer have a naively optimistic view of human society and the role of business therein; they see CSV as mostly a win-win scenario in which companies, by taking on projects which will create value for society or wide ranges of stakeholders, will also be led to be more profitable. This will also push them to be more aligned on regulation. To be precise, Porter and Kramer (2011) first assume corporate compliance and then argue that the wide acceptance of CSV will increase alignment between businesses and governments on regulation in many areas. Put another way, Porter and Kramer do not see any trade-off between profitability and pursuing a socially responsible approach to business contributing to social progress. This consideration of social needs[1] (only) as a source of a greater and shared creation of value may effectively be accused of naive optimism because they do not explicitly consider possible win-lose situations, which are probably more typical.

However, curiously, in the light of the clarification of the meaning of value which we have proposed in the previous chapter, perhaps, the Porter-Kramer position gains considerably in strength and plausibility. There is only one value (net addition to human well-being), and businesses to be profitable should and will seek to create this value since, apart from scamming and outright fraud, such value creation remains the key to profitability (this last being the *fruit* of successful value creation).

Behind the obsession with the trade-off (or, conversely, the integration) between economic and social value, another question rumbles: the *distribution* of the value created. With CSV, for whom in society is value increased and how much for each? On this question, Porter and Kramer remain essentially silent. They seem to assume that in a potential win-win CSV situation where value is created, nobody will be too worried about the distribution of the gains. Herein if anywhere, lies the naivety of their stance. In a win-win situation, there will certainly be net gains, and all stakeholders could potentially be made better off, but how much everyone will be made better off depends on the distribution of the shared value created.

Moreover, all too many real-world situations (including many which could *potentially* be win-win) are, in practice, win-lose, as just remarked above. The difficulty here is, in fact, closely analogous to that already familiar to economists in international trade theory and welfare economics as potential Pareto improvement. A *Pareto improvement* is a socio-economic change that leaves some people better off while leaving nobody worse off. In other words, given our definition of value, it creates an increase in value for multiple people with no decrease in value for anyone. Now most socio-economic changes, and certainly those we may have to consider in the context of a business endeavouring to create shared value, involve, in the distribution of the spoils, gains for some stakeholders and losses for others; and in such cases, we cannot speak of a Pareto improvement. If, however, the gains of the gainers outweigh the losses of the losers, we can speak of a *potential* Pareto improvement in the precise sense that the gainers could afford wholly to compensate the losers and still remain better off. In short, the potential Pareto improvement could be transformed into an actual real Pareto improvement by the gainers taking steps to compensate all losers fully.

The trouble with the capitalist system is not in respect of its ability to unleash massive value creation (a point which even Marx himself acknowledged) but instead in the presumption that the whole or the vast bulk of the value created should accrue to capitalist owners (shareholders) rather than to other stakeholder groups. That, however, is not an economic necessity but merely a political and/or legal (corporate governance) choice: it is purely ideological and reflective of the power relations in a society. It is, moreover, a hot potato on which Porter and Kramer do not comment. If there is a certain naivety and failure to recognise tensions in Porter and Kramer's position, it is then here on the distributional question, not in the shared value conception itself. Thus they simply avoid the vexed distributional question that is lurking beneath the false dichotomy of 'economic value' and 'social value'. For them, the crucial challenge is to get the shared value created: discussions and squabbles about value capture and the distribution of the shared value are secondary and can come afterwards. This, in turn, explains the apparent optimism that pervades their article and which Crane et al. (2014) have described as naive. It is indeed perhaps a trifle optimistic to assume away the distributional questions and trade-offs, but Porter and Kramer are by no means the only economists to do so. One has only to consider the discussions of classic comparative cost advantage theories by economists to find a very similar optimism which, while demonstrating the potential for an increase in world output through specialisation in accordance with comparative advantage, shies away from distributional questions.

Nevertheless, it would be churlish not to say that it is deeply mistaken to reject multilateral free trade and to retract into protectionism just because of issues with the distribution of the gains. To do so means (just as necessarily as the freeing of trade increases world output from a given resource set) to reduce overall world output from the same resources. There is no chance of a win-win from protectionism; there *must* be losers.

There is something similar in the relative optimism of Porter and Kramer in respect of creating shared value. By concentrating on creating shared value, by 'reconnecting company success with social progress' (Porter & Kramer, 2011, p. 62), companies can create a potential win-win where manifold stakeholders in a society can experience gains. Indeed, they assert that 'profits involving a social purpose represent a higher form of capitalism, one that will enable society to advance more rapidly while allowing companies to grow even more. The result is a positive cycle of company and community prosperity' (Porter & Kramer, 2011, p. 75). Whether this positive cycle materialises into a real win-win depends on the distributional question in respect of those gains, a question which, while important, is for them essentially secondary, even a kind of political no-go area. The priority, as with free trade, is to create shared value in the first place.

4.2 Philosophical roots of optimism and pessimism

Given the optimism which pervades the Porter/Kramer outlook (whether naive or not), it will be interesting to investigate further the ultimate philosophical and economic roots of such optimism. This will lead us into a brief aside on the philosophy of history and to a re-examination of the much-abused notion of rationality in economics. We will show that the two sides in the CSV controversy have very different but unstated presuppositions in respect of such themes and that this, moreover, explains why the discussion between the protagonists can often seem like 'ships that pass in the night'.

From Marx's work on dialectical materialism (as a philosophy of history) we may take over a picture of human history as a constant economic struggle to get maximum output in terms of material well-being from resources which are cruelly limited in relation to the goals to which people aspire. This is, of course, the central problem of Economics as a discipline[2] and will be recognised as the challenge of value creation (in the basic meaning of that term: adding to human well-being). But we would suggest that there are two primordial ways in which this problem of scarcity can be approached and resolved by human beings. The first is what we may call an acquisitive antagonistic approach in which groups of individuals seek to arrogate for themselves the lion's share, if not all of the scarce resources available and to exclude (largely or entirely) those outside of the privileged group from the enjoyment of the fruits of those scarce resources. The aggressor group, recognising the problem of scarcity of means in relation to material aspirations, strikes pre-emptively to guarantee material abundance for itself. If that means that others outside the aggressors' privileged circle suffer deprivation and destitution, then so be it. As luminaries of this approach would argue, there will always be losers[3] (Nietzsche, 1990/1889; Rand, 1999). This aggressively acquisitive stance can be expressed in social class dominance (as in Marx's system), or it could be expressed as caste dominance, racial dominance or through a nationalistic or imperialistic/colonialist dominance (see Marx, 1976/1887; Cornforth, 1953) or in our own day sometimes as oligarchic dominance of all stripes. At its most brutal, it is the master-slave dialectic. In fact, when we recognise the commonalities among the various forms which the acquisitive antagonistic approach can take and reduce them in this way, we might argue that what has been taken in the past to be distinct interpretations of human history and human conflicts ultimately boil down to essentially one basic form of conflict motivated by the individualist greed of the 'masters', the aggressors in the master-slave relationship. We are not here seeking to be reductionist for its own sake or seeking to simplify the processes of history; we are simply noting on reflection a commonality among a variety of different forms of social conflict which have usually been interpreted independently of each other (although there are some hints of the centrality of the master-slave dialectic to be found in the more recondite corners of the thought of Hegel and of Jean-Paul Sartre) (Hegel, 1977/1807; Sartre, 1956, Part 3).

The second primordial approach which we can detect in human history is what we call a cooperative synthetic, one in which human beings over some defined area explicitly recognise their interdependence and their shared aspirations; and instead of acting towards each other in a self-centred acquisitive and inevitably antagonistic manner which will, in the end, be self-defeating for many if not all of those concerned, they agree to cooperate to get the best possible result for all. The result (it is hoped) will be a harmonious and peaceful society, at least in the area where the cooperation occurs. It is worth emphasising that if everyone acts in a greedily acquisitive manner in the face of scarcity of resources, there are bound to be those who will be disappointed, and one may even reach a result which is bad for all in the event that those who lose out in the materialist rat race decide to take matters into their own hands to redistribute the scarce resources by more or less violent means (social breakdown, criminality, and in extreme cases social revolutions).

For the protagonists of cooperation, when people face common problems in which the realisation of their goals and aspirations are interdependent (for example, with climate change in our day), cooperation in the face of the challenges is the most, if not in some cases, the only *rational* solution. This insight runs counter to a long tradition of thinking in a narrowly individualistic manner about rationality in respect of human action and which has come to be known as '*rational economic man*' or '*homo economicus*'. Rational economic men and women are portrayed as ruthlessly self-seeking individuals who further their own narrow self-interests at all costs and in all situations, who are incapable of recognising the implications of commonly shared problems and for whom it is inconceivable that the well-being of others might actually be an argument in their utility functions. In short, they are incapable of compassion, let alone the love of others. We are not perhaps the first to remark on the total obliteration of feelings of sympathy and empathy in the rational economic men and women supposed to be the actors at the heart of the economic system; but, once we recognise our shared destinies, those actors are not only devoid of feeling, they are downright irrational as well. The epithet 'irrational economic men and women' would be more appropriate certainly today if not indeed always.

This recognition of interdependence lies, of course, at the heart of the political philosophies of Aristotle (man is a political animal) and of all the social contract theorists Hobbes, Locke, Rousseau, and Rawls, each in their own way (for a summary of social contract theory see Boucher & Kelly, 1994). If the driving force behind social contract theories is the notion of a hypothetical state of nature without government in which anarchy prevails and in which, at least for Hobbes, this anarchy will lead to a 'war of all against all' in which the life of people in such a state of nature will be 'solitary poor nasty brutish and short' this hypothetical state would apply as much to businesses as social organisations of people just as much as to individuals in a state of nature (Hobbes, 1969/1651, p. 143). Therefore, the solution to the unsatisfactory and, for Hobbes, highly undesirable state of anarchy is to enter into a (hypothetical) social contract whereby all individuals and we can now say also all businesses and social organisations will surrender their rights to a sovereign government charged with delivering a peaceful, harmonious (and one hopes also prosperous) society. Social organisations of all kinds can thus be deemed to be corporate citizens to which the sovereign government emerging from the hypothetical social contract will accord various rights, and of course, going with these rights, there will be social responsibilities (just as individuals will have certain civic responsibilities), and a primary responsibility for both individual and corporate citizens of any kind will be to pay taxes. One can hardly expect to have all of the advantages of a stable government that preserves the peace and restricts criminality without paying for these. Speaking in particular of business as a social institution and community of persons (created and formed by humans and for them), any business is historically endowed with the potential both to conflict and/or to cooperate with other social actors. The uncertainty that characterises it as a socio-economic system, complex, open, dynamic and (if profitable) enduring (von Bertalanffy, 1968) may be addressed either by antagonistic or by cooperative behaviour or both in combination.

Porter and Kramer and those who enthusiastically follow their approach implicitly adopt a cooperative synthetic view of human affairs and history. Some would say to the point of naivety, they are optimistic about the possibilities of creating shared value, and they minimise the tensions (which, as we have seen, are in any case about the distribution rather than the creation of shared value). To Porter and Kramer, it is just rational and evident that businesses should cooperate with all other social actors to create social progress:

> The concept of shared value can be defined as policies and operating practices that enhance the competitiveness of a company while simultaneously advancing the economic and social conditions in the communities in which it operates. Shared value creation focuses on identifying and expanding the connections between societal and economic progress.
>
> (Porter & Kramer, 2011, p. 66)

Shining through this and the similar manifold assertions made by Porter and Kramer that is a decidedly cooperative synthetic view. For them, it is ridiculous and irrational to set up an antagonism between business and society: business is in and must collaborate with society and all of its actors. Porter (2000, 2003) is, of course, also well-known for his work on industrial clusters, which he sees as the foundation of competitiveness and the economic development of regions: but industrial clusters are again based on a degree of collaboration between companies in a particular sector, trade organisations and local or national government officials and agencies which can facilitate cluster development. Finally, it may come as a surprise to some, but Porter (Porter & Kramer, 2011; Porter, 2019) also insists on a cooperative relationship between business and government, seen as the ultimate regulator of the economy: 'Regulation is necessary for well-functioning markets, something that became abundantly clear during the recent financial crisis. However, the ways in which regulations are designed and implemented determine whether they benefit society or work against it' (Porter & Kramer, 2011, p. 74). Therefore, whereas in the past, the focus of Porter's work was almost exclusively on the competitiveness of firms, there is detectable in his work on clusters, on CSV and on social progress a definite shift towards a position which gives a place also to cooperation in the broadest sense seen as an eminently rational approach to human challenges. Porter and Kramer may not have articulated such a synthetic cooperative view in philosophical terms, but we would suggest that they are certainly in sympathy with such a philosophy. More specifically (and again though they do not articulate it as such), they are very much in line with the basic insights that are shared in all of the social contract political philosophies: that in the face of the disorder, predations and dangers of anarchy (state of nature) human beings will (or hypothetically would) come together, rationally recognising their interdependence to form collaboratively at the very least a state with government and laws to protect individuals and their property rights (Lockean version of the social contract), if not an all-powerful sovereign (as in Hobbes' version). When Porter and Kramer speak of the indispensable role of regulation of markets (as just quoted above), they are perhaps closer to a Hobbesian rather than a Lockean take on the social contract, but that is a minor detail of exegesis since in their actual article Porter and Kramer do not actually mention social contract.

For their part, Crane et al. and many other critics of the CSV concept are operating with a much more antagonistic acquisitive conception of human society and history more closely related to but not reducible to Marx's dialectical materialism. To be fair and clear, most of the critics of CSV would not defend for one moment the latent supremacist claims (based on class, caste, race, etc.) that necessarily underpin such a conception of human interactions in society and their ethical critiques are designed precisely to alleviate the tensions in an antagonistic world. Nevertheless, they regard the antagonisms and related acquisitive greed as inevitable, and they would see cooperative synthetic scenarios for humanity as naive idealism or, worse, a manipulative managerial strategy. To quote Crane et al. (2014, p. 136):

> Many corporate decisions related to social and environmental problems, however creative the decision-maker may be, do not present themselves as potential win-win but rather will manifest themselves in terms of dilemmas. In an ethical dilemma world views, identities, interests and values collide.

Furthermore, they argue that 'Porter and Kramer claim to move beyond any such trade-offs, largely it would appear by ignoring them' (Crane et al., 2014, p. 136) but ultimately 'CSV is naive about the challenges of business compliance and based on a shallow conception of the role of the corporation in society' (Crane et al., 2014, p. 131). Or even

In many respects, the CSV concept is actually just as corporate-centric as Porter's 'old' strategy models. It explains how the corporation can transform (some) of its social and environmental problems into win-win solutions. In this sense, it largely follows the logic of the traditional model of competitive strategy, which demands that corporations establish barriers against the market entry of competitors.

(Crane et al., 2014, p. 141)

It is clear enough from these and many other statements that while they might grudgingly admire the essentially cooperative synthetic vision of the role of business in society that is held out by CSV, they regard it as naively idealistic (or opportunistic), in effect because humanity will never be capable of shaking off the antagonistic acquisitive tendencies of certain groups or classes; and as a result human life will be a constant conflict, a never-ending power struggle between antagonistic self-interests; between in particular businesses (represented by their shareholders) and society, although the antagonistic approach can even be present within the same company. An example is 'the best-alternative test' (Goold et al., 1994), which proposed to select the business with the greatest internal advantage for the corporate portfolio in a multi-business company.[4] But it is also clear that what they are depicting is, in effect, a pre-social contract world in which narrow self-interests reign supreme as people and corporate entities give themselves over to a 'war of all against all', as described by Hobbes and in which there is no awareness of the possible rationality of cooperation.

4.3 Towards a rationally founded optimism

Given that the roots of the antagonistic acquisitive vision of human affairs and history are strongly associated with the conception of 'rational economic man' that has been widely prevalent, especially in classical and neo-classical economics, it will be interesting to see the way in which this presumption has become so deeply rooted in the discipline of Economics despite the fact that as we have seen it is decidedly challengeable on philosophical grounds. Peter Fleming (Fleming, 2017) has outlined the widespread influence of the idea of rational economic men and women (*homo economicus*) over two centuries of economic theorising and has shown its severe limitations as an explanation of human interaction in the economic sphere. Yet, despite the evident limitations, the concept continues to be given a central place in Microeconomics, and so Fleming suggests that a major reason for the persistence of the concept is essentially ideological: it is an essential premise for the edifice of neoclassical economics based on the ideas of utility maximising individuals and profit-maximising firms to stand up and to reach its characteristic market fundamentalist conclusions.[5] We may add to Fleming's cogently argued thesis a very telling specific example from the microeconomic theory of oligopoly: the (supposed) prisoners dilemma game.

In oligopoly markets, where there is a small number of big firms present in the market, each firm, in defining its strategy, must take into account the likely reactions of other firms in the market; there is a high degree of strategic interdependence. Such interdependence is not found in monopolies because there are no direct competitors present in the market, while in what economists call 'perfect' competition (large numbers of firms producing a homogeneous good), there are so many competing firms in the market that no firm has any leeway to change prices or to define its own strategy (in the absence of any product differentiation). Strategic interdependence is, therefore, exclusively a feature of oligopolies for economists. In such a market, when firms adopt a specific strategy, they must recognise that this will impact the other firms in the market, particularly if a specific strategic move by a firm significantly increases its market share and profitability. The other firms can therefore be expected to react to the first firm's moves, but that reaction can only be guessed at by the first firm.

Nevertheless, the success of this or that strategy beyond the immediate short term depends critically on how exactly the competing firms react. Hence each oligopoly firm, in deciding on its strategy, must make guesses as to how the other firms are likely to react and base their own strategies on this expectation. Strategic interdependence in oligopoly not only, therefore, introduces a considerable degree of uncertainty into such markets; they also have all of the characteristics of any competitive game. We have a variety of actors in competition with each other where each one will base their own strategy on their best guesses as to how the others will 'play the (oligopoly) game'.

In this way, economists have been led to apply the broader theory of games to the understanding of oligopoly markets, sometimes in the form of quite sophisticated mathematical models. One such model, which is decidedly unsophisticated but widely taught in Microeconomics courses and can be found in many Economics textbooks, is the prisoner's Dilemma game. It is extremely revealing in the way it has been used by economists.

In the Prisoners Dilemma (see, for example, Sloman & Wride, 2009), we have two prisoners who are suspected of implication in a crime, and we are asked to consider the likelihood of getting an outright admission of guilt that could lead to a definitive conviction. There are minor variations in the way that the game is set up, but the essentials remain the same in all versions: communication between the 'prisoners' is impossible, and, therefore, the pursuit of narrow self-interest prevents a superior cooperative solution from being reached. Both of the prisoners were actually involved in the crime, but the evidence is very much circumstantial, and so to get a conviction, one or the other or both of them would have to make a confession of guilt for prosecutors to be able to get a definitive conviction. If one confesses while the other does not, that prisoner can expect a degree of leniency from the authorities. The prisoners, however, are strictly separated and cannot in any way communicate with each other, so neither knows how the other will react under interrogation. In this relatively stilted scenario, we are asked to consider what would be the most rational strategy for each prisoner to adopt under interrogation. If both admit the crime, they each get reduced sentences. If one admits while the other denies, the denier gets a full sentence, while the admitter gets a much reduced sentence or even a pardon. If both deny, neither can be sentenced, and they will both go free. Assuming that they would each prefer to go free rather than be in prison and given the key presumption of the game that they cannot communicate or liaise in any way, then the rational action would be for each one to confess to the crime. This is analogous to the Nash equilibrium of the more formal models of oligopoly.

But that is within the highly stilted conditions of the supposed game. It is surely self-evident that if such a situation arose in reality, by far, the most rational thing for each prisoner to do would be to do everything in their power to try to communicate so that they could each agree to deny the crime under interrogation and thus both go free. In short, the most rational solution, in reality, would be for each prisoner to recognise their interdependence and cooperate in search of the jointly optimal solution. What is highly revealing in all of this is that economists have set up this game in a way that a priori rules out any possibility of cooperation. Such a move, given that it is manifest that in a real-world situation the prisoners would seek by every means to liaise and cooperate, is purely ideological: economists entirely wedded to the idea of rational economic man (and woman) as totally isolated individuals maximising their own self-interest ruthlessly are completely blinkered to the possible rationality of cooperation. They dare not admit that people might actually recognise their interdependence and agree rationally to cooperate for the common good. An unreconstructed *homo economicus* fundamentalist might retort that even if the prisoners can liaise and see the advantages of both denying the crime, neither one can be sure, even after communication and agreeing on the double denial, that each will go through with it when the interrogation happens. That is always a possibility but, in this case, quite unlikely given the manifest gains for both if they both deny the crime. But if one is to try to build one's life in human societies on the presumption that other people will systematically lie, then as the liar paradoxes have anciently shown, human communication and, therefore, any possibility of a socialised existence (let alone of business) break down totally and completely. Actually, the purveyors of the *homo economicus* myth are probably more than anything else holding up proudly to the world a not very flattering entirely self-centred avaricious and greedy self-portrait in which they presume everyone else in the world is like them. In fact, if they cannot bring themselves to see that people can over significant areas trust each other and hence cooperate, they should, consistently, retire as hermits to a desert island Robinson Crusoe style. It is actually no accident that many market fundamentalist ideologues do indeed dream of retiring to some kind of brand new anarcho-capitalist supposed paradise on remote islands in the Pacific ... usually however not quite as Robinson Crusoe but surrounded rather by like-minded anarcho-capitalists whom ironically they might even be prepared to trust!

These are indeed harsh words, but in the face of blinkered obstinacy, they are sometimes needed to awaken certain thinkers from their ideological dreams and self-contradictions. In any case, we believe that we have shown clearly the rationality of cooperation in pursuit of common goals; and that the narrow individualist conception of rational economic men and women that has for two centuries been peddled by neoclassical and market fundamentalist economists is implausible, blinkered to the reality of the significance of cooperation and trust among human beings if life in society is to be possible; and ultimately its function is that of an ideological myth for said market fundamentalists.[6]

Notes

1 The topic has not been explored here; instead, it was left implied. Nevertheless, it is worth remembering that the ability to create value also depends on how social needs are met, therefore, by how the CSV strategy is put into practice. In addition, the chosen production combination also impacts the relationship between value and profit.

2 One immediately thinks of Lionel Robbins (1932) classic definition of the subject: 'Economics is a discipline which studies human actions as a relationship between ends and scarce means which have alternative uses'. Robbins, L. (1932). *An essay on the nature and significance of Economic Science*. London: Macmillan.

3 Luminaries would here include the philosopher Nietzsche, the anarcho-capitalist Ayn Rand and perhaps not-so-luminary former US president Donald Trump.

4 Porter himself, in 1987, pioneered this vision with 'the better-off test', then superseded by his subsequent writings and the CSV concept itself. Specifically, he identified three empirical tests to be formulated to determine whether or not a diversification strategy can bring a competitive advantage. Among these, the better-off test allows identifying whether two units or companies would be more profitable if combined into a single unit or company. See Porter, M.E. (1987). From competitive advantage to corporate strategy. *Harvard Business Review*, May/June, 43–59.

5 To this day, the second author of the book can still recall a telling exchange he had some twenty years ago in a seminar discussion with a leading British market fundamentalist. He had posed the perhaps cheeky question at a certain juncture in the exchanges as to what ultimately was the source of human well-being or, more concretely, what is the ultimate purpose of human activity in the world: the reply he received was '*to make more money*'.

6 The second author has argued elsewhere that a very similar mythical function in market fundamentalist ideology can be attributed to the Capital Asset Pricing Model and Efficient Markets Hypothesis. Both

continue to be widely upheld by fundamentalists despite their manifest falsification as a description of financial market realities. Their
function is essentially ideological. See O'Sullivan, P. (2018). The capital asset pricing model and the efficient markets hypothesis: the compelling fairy tale of contemporary financial economics. *International
Journal of Political Economy*, *47*(3–4), 225–52.

References

Boucher, D., & Kelly, P. (Eds.). (1994). *The social contract from Hobbes to
Rawls*. London: Routledge.
Brandenburger, A., & Harborne, S. (1996). Value-based business strategy.
Journal of Economics and Management Strategy, *50*, 5–24
Cornforth, M. (1953). *Dialectical materialism*. New York: International
Publishers.
Crane, A., Palazzo, G., Spence, L.J., & Matten, D. (2014). Contesting the
value of 'creating shared value'. *California Management Review*, *56*(2),
130–53.
Dobb, M. (1973). *Theories of value and distribution since Adam
Smith: ideology and economic theory*. Cambridge: Cambridge
University Press.
Fleming, P. (2017). *The death of homo economicus*. London: Pluto Press.
Goold, M.C., Campbell A., & Alexander M. (1994). *Corporate-
level strategy: creating value in the multibusiness company*.
New York: Wiley.
Hegel, G.W.F. (1977). *Phenomoenology of mind*, translated by Miller, A.,
with Introduction by Findlay, J. Oxford: Clarendon Press (original
work first published in 1807).
Hobbes, T. (1969). *Leviathan*. London: Fontana Paperbacks. (Original
work first published in 1651.)
Marx, K. (1976). *Capital*, Vol 1. London: Penguin Books. (Original work
first published in English 1887.)
Myrdal, G. (1959). *Value in social theory*. London: Routledge.
Nietzsche, F. (1990). *Twilight of the idols*. Penguin Classic. London: Penguin
Books. (Original work published 1889.)
O'Sullivan, P. (2018). The capital asset pricing model and the efficient
markets hypothesis: the compelling fairy tale of contemporary financial
economics. *International Journal of Political Economy*, *47*(3–4), 225–52.
Pitelis, C.N. (2009). The co-evolution of organizational value capture,
value creation and sustainable advantage. *Organization Studies*, *30*(10),
1115–39.
Porter, M.E. (1987). From competitive advantage to corporate strategy.
Harvard Business Review, May/June, 43–59.

Porter, M.E. (2000). Location, competition, and economic development: local clusters in a global economy. *Economic Development Quarterly*, *14*(1), 15–34.

Porter, M.E. (2003). The economic performance of regions. *Regional Studies*, *37*(6–7), 549–78.

Porter, M.E. (2019). TED talk on Creating Shared Value. Retrieved from www.ted.com/talks/michael_porter_the_case_for_letting_business_so lve_social_problems?sf18068809=1#t-972150

Porter, M.E., & Kramer, M. (2011). Creating Shared Value. *Harvard Business Review*, *89*(1), 62–77.

Rand, A. (1999). *Return of the primitive: the anti-industrial revolution.* New York: Plume. (Retitled edition of Rand, A. (1971). *The New Left: the anti-industrial revolution.*)

Robbins, L. (1932). *An essay on the nature and significance of Economic Science.* London: Macmillan.

Sartre, J.P. (1956). *Being and nothingness.* London: Routledge.

Sloman, J., & Wride, A. (2009). *Economics* (7th ed.). Harlow: Pearson Prentice-Hall.

von Bertalanffy, L. (1968). *General system theory: foundations, development, applications.* New York: George Braziller.

5 Concluding reflections

In this book, we have proposed a philosophical analysis of the elusive notion of value used in Economics and various other Management disciplines and related this to the rationality in action studied in these disciplines and to the philosophy of history. The particular trigger for this exegesis was the heated debate that has occurred in the field of strategic management and business ethics theory around the concept of Creating Shared Value (CSV) which Porter and Kramer (2011) have argued to be indispensable if a free market system, based on capitalist free enterprise, aims to survive what they see as a growing crisis of legitimacy. Surprisingly, this seemingly laudable position has generated a great deal of controversy (e.g. Crane et al., 2014, Porter & Kramer, 2014). It seemed to us that among the reasons for the stand-off were probably lurking some fundamental differences in the implicit economic and philosophical presuppositions of theorists on all sides. Our purpose was not so much to take sides in the vexed debate but rather to lay bare some of the hidden positions and assumptions being made on all sides, in particular, in respect of the notions of value, rationality, and the philosophy of history. Upon a precise philosophical analysis, we argued that in the case of value, the ultimate core of shared meaning/signification of this term across all of its various uses is the idea of the *net addition to human well-being*. What is valuable is that it leads to an increase in well-being in the broadest sense (and not just in a narrow utilitarian sense). We went on to note that the contrast in the debates about CSV between economic and social value involves a false dichotomy since, ultimately, the creation of value is about the enhancement of human well-being,

DOI: 10.4324/9781003398943-5

and the supposed dichotomy is not about two different kinds of value creation but rather hinges on somewhat different views about the most appropriate distribution of the value created by private enterprise firms; in short, it concerns value capture and not value creation. We also showed that the supposed dichotomy implicitly sees business (with its creation of 'economic value') as somehow disjointed from human society when, in fact, businesses are irrevocably in and a key part of human societies with the result that such value they create (additions to human well-being) constitutes necessarily a part of 'social value'.

Having shown that the debate cannot ultimately be about the creation of two opposing types of value, we went on to suggest that the bitter opposition between protagonists in the CSV debate reflects differences in their ultimate views of the philosophy of history. On the one hand, the opponents of CSV take a pessimistic view of human history as being essentially a constant struggle for power among social groups in which dominant groups with supremacist pretensions seek to arrogate for themselves the lion's share of the world's scarce resources and the value that can be created from these. This antagonistic conception may be played out based on social class, race, religion, or other presumed supremacist rights. This may be contrasted with a cooperative synthetic view of human affairs in which all people recognise their inherent interdependence and agree in the face of scarcity (and other even more severe challenges such as pandemics or climate change) to cooperate to get a solution which is best for all. This cooperative view involves a much more optimistic vision of human affairs and potential. It shines through clearly as an implicit presumption of the defenders of the CSV approach with its central idea of creating value through business in a manner that simultaneously contributes to well-being across a wide range of stakeholders and, thus, to social progress.

Nevertheless, having exposed these presuppositions in the CSV debate, we wondered if we could map a way forward from the opposition or, in terms of Hegelian dialectical logic, pass beyond the antithesis phase of the argumentation towards a new synthesis. Attempting to provide an answer led us to a recalibration of the notion of rationality as used (or abused) by economists.

Given the possibility and indeed the historical existence of the antagonistic and the cooperative approaches, we would argue that the only rational response – as well as the morally more accept-able one – for intelligent, critically rational human beings, is to cooperate at all levels: microeconomic cooperation at the level of the individual business enterprise (creating shared value); macro level (indeed world level) cooperation in respect of macroeco-nomic challenges such as climate change; and supranational pol-itical cooperation as the necessary framework to give effect to all of this. If we use the loaded words 'only rational response', it is because of the inescapable and undeniable fact of the interdepend-ence of human activities and destinies in our world. If practical rationality in human action consists at the very least in taking in some or whatever sense the means deemed most effective to the attainment of our goals and well-being, logically, it must start *inter alia* from a recognition that, in almost all of our practical activities in the world, we are in part dependent on the actions and destinies of various of our fellow human beings. In fact, in the early twenty-first century, with extensive trade and free movement of capital, increasingly free movement of labour and almost instant commu-nication with every corner of the globe via the Internet, the inter-dependence of humanity in the face of the challenges of scarcity is evident and, indeed, during the Covid-19 pandemic agonisingly driven home.

In the face of such interdependence, humankind is more than ever in need of a cooperative synthetic approach to the challenges of scarcity. Therefore, we would characterise it as the only rational response because it is the only properly effective response to our contemporary political and economic policy challenges. This per-spective is also increasingly accepted in managerial studies, both in the public and private domains. It has progressively led to the development of new frameworks and constructs, such as the value constellation (Normann & Ramírez, 1993), co-production, and co-generation of value, as theorised in the literature of public choice (Ostrom, 1996) or co-production and co-creation of value, as theorised in strategic management/service literature (Vargo et al., 2008). Moreover, the studies on public value have focused on overcoming economic individualism, also stressed in public policy, to affirm the importance of the interdependence between public and private interests and the needed transition from government to governance (Moore, 1995; Bozeman, 2007). In this direction, we may also mention the work of Mahoney et al. (2009) concerned with the interdependence of public and private interests, which suggests an alternative criterion to evaluate the consequences of economic activities for private and public welfare, i.e. global (= world community) sustainable (= long-term enduring perspective) value creation (= cost-benefits of activities); the interdependence of human destinies throughout the world thus becomes central to the discussion of business and public policy.

The antagonistic acquisitive approach in our interdependent world could be rationally coherent for this or that dominant group only if the group adopts some supremacist claim, be it racial, religious, nationalistic, plutocratic or otherwise, which would allow that group both morally (as somehow a matter of moral right) and practically to ignore and ride roughshod over the interests and aspirations of other lesser sections of humanity. Although it may seem a somewhat daring and, for some, a problematic assertion, we would venture to suggest, however, that no such supremacist claim has ever stood up to philosophical or scientific scrutiny and so has ever had a rational or scientific foundation (Gillie, 1977; Buchanan, 2010; Marks, 2019). That has not prevented human history from being littered with the conflicts set in motion by supremacist claims and pre-emption of scarce resources based on such claims, and indeed most of human history could be seen as antagonistic, with just rare periods when cooperative synthetic views have timidly and to a degree taken hold in certain parts of the world.

Effectively, in examining the contemporary world, if, on the one hand, we observe what we have defined as an inexorably increasing interdependence in the challenges to humanity (which would suggest an increasingly optimistic and cooperative view of society), on the other hand, we cannot fail to take into account a countervailing set of tendencies which could be seen to be pointing towards an increasingly antagonistic view. Quite apart from the various wars, more or less declared, violent or commercial, which are still in progress, it is necessary to draw attention to a recent trend, which could open up dark scenarios.

In the introduction, we referred to the strong push towards business models (including CSV) that go beyond the traditional model of profit at any cost, even to the detriment of consumers, the community, and the environment. While academics and others are trying to be convincing about the need to humanise businesses, i.e. to put people back at the centre of business decisions and policies (Freeman et al., 2020), the role of technology and big data is becoming more and more pervasive. Therefore, while we chase old ethical problems and dilemmas with solutions and correctives not yet fully implemented, the capitalist system seems to be at a new turning point, which opens up new possibilities, but also new dangers: companies – and the overall society – have entirely revised their relationship with technology, which has become the engine of the capitalist system. Zuboff's bestseller highlights how globalised big corporations are increasingly capable of almost wholly controlling every human behaviour (Zuboff, 2019). Other studies and experiences also point in this direction and demonstrate a deep interest towards controlling feelings and behaviours not only of companies but also of States (Chin & Lin, 2022). All this highlights the distinction, but we could also talk about separation, between profit and value and how it is still absolutely current. To what extent does tracking behaviours and preferences create value, and what is the breaking point from which such a policy becomes a sinister pursuit of profit (e.g. pushing consumers to buy more and more) with no creation of value? After all, digital manipulation is creating wants and a sensation of inadequacy or deprivation (so, reduction of well-being) in order that the perceived inadequacies can then be profitably met by unscrupulous businesses (think of the impact of influencers, especially on adolescents, through social media). In such a sequence, there is no net creation of value at all. The idea that consumer wants are manipulated for business gain through increased sales of various products or services is not, of course, new; but in the era of the Internet and social media, it has taken on a new dimension; and in the context of our argument in this work, it underlines very clearly the untenability of the sloppy tendency to equate value and profitability.

The discrepancy between value and profitability is also exposed by other scholars who demonstrate how technology-enabled productive activities have become all-encompassing under a managerial and social profile (Pasquale, 2015).

Starting and then going beyond Zuboff's considerations, it is possible to glimpse, as a possible scenario, an even more complex future based on a power that radicalises and focuses exclusively on the holder of data, in their management and in their processing to generate profits. We could call this *'radical power control'* or *'algorithmic control'*, whose boundaries are summarised in Table 5.1.

Table 5.1 A possible scenario: from totalitarianism to algorithmical power

Three species of power

Comparative elements	Totalitarianism	Instrumentarianism	Algorithmical
Central metaphor	Big Brother	Big Other	Big Data
Totalistic vision	Total Possession	Total Certainty	Total Control
Transcendent purpose	Perfection of Society/Species Defined by Class or Race	Automation of Market/Society for the Certainty of Guaranteed Outcomes	Algorithm Supremacy
Locus of power	Control of the Means of Violence	Control of the Division of Learning in Society	Control of the Division of Knowledge in Society
Means of power	Hierarchical Administration of Terror	Ownership of the Means of Behavioural Modification	Data Property
Foundational mechanism	Arbitrary Terror; Murder	Dispossession of Behavioural Surplus for Computation, Control, Prediction	Pain and Artificial Intelligence
Theory and practice	Theory Legitimates Practice	Practice Conceals Theory	Practice Can Do Without Theory
Ideological style	Political Religion	Radical Indifference	Denial of Any Ideology
Social strategies	Atomisation and Division; Total Believers Or Total Enemies	Otherisation Of Predictable Organisms	From Individual To Dividual
Core social processes	In-Group, Out-Group for Conformity and Obedience	Hive Mind; Social Comparison For Confluence And Predictability	Addiction to the Condition

(*Continued*)

Table 5.1 (Continued)

Three species of power

Comparative elements	Totalitarianism	Instrumentarianism	Algorithmical
Unit of social production	Mass (Political)	Population (Statistical)	Dollop (Sociological)
Vector of social influence	'Re-Education' Exerts Control From Inside-Out	Behavioural Modification Exerts Control From Outside-In	Self-Learning and Surveillance
Social patterning	Radical Isolation	Radical Connection	Malleable Dividuo
Demands on individual	Absolute Loyalty Through Subjugation to State/Species	Absolute Transparency Through Subjugation To Guaranteed Outcomes	Absolute Trust in the Algorithmic System
Primary source of individual attachment to power	Thwarted Identity	Thwarted Effectiveness	Annihilation of the Ability to Think for Oneself
Primary mode of individual attachment to power	Identification	Dependency	Exclusion

Source: Authors' adaptation from Zuboff (2019, pp. 372–3).

The central metaphor is given by the idea that everything is governable, from feelings to social behaviours, by means of (big) data, according to how these are collected and used. The vision is that of total control of each individual and each community. Data ownership is the main goal for companies; data is, at the same time, a condition for generating wealth and wealth itself. This is entrepreneurially possible through the supremacy of algorithms and the concentration of economic power over data ownership. Artificial intelligence is achievable only by using data that feeds precise algorithms, through which it could also be possible to control fears and anxieties. The relationship between theory and practice is transformed, with an evident prevalence of the second over the first: it is not necessary to elaborate theories but to adapt practice to the needs of the construction of shareholder value (profitability) that companies intend to achieve. In this context, ideologies continue to lose their meaning; better to do without them, better to do without an ideological complexity capable only of hindering the production of profits and so of shareholder material wealth. The strategy of society is no longer based on the individual as an integral indivisible subject but on the individual as a subject that can be decomposed, lacking in its critical conscience and susceptible to manipulation. This individual can then be called indeed *dividuo*[1] as opposed to *individuo* (in Italian). Thus, it is easier to build desires and needs, to manipulate them. This increases dependencies and inequalities and makes the ability to organise collective responses much more complex. In this scenario, consumption, a necessary premise to achieve productive combinations capable of generating wealth, is obtained by self-learning and surveillance of behaviour in a kind of spiral. The malleable *dividuo* represents well the social patterning that emerges, with absolute confidence in algorithms and technological systems considered superior to human intelligence. In this direction, a gradual downsizing begins until the ability to reason alone and with one's own mind gradually disappears. In short, individual freedom of choice in decision-making is progressively annihilated.

We cannot know whether this (fearsome) future will become a reality or remain just one of the plausible distant scenarios devoid of materialisation. On the other hand, among these scenarios, one could also include a society that, however technological, has managed to raise humanity to its nth degree, a society based on cooperation and the power of human reasoning rather than on the algorithmic aimed at dehumanisation. Regardless of our future, our argument can stay the same. The dreaded world based on the power of data would be just another page of history governed by an antagonist vision, but that does not change the observation that it is irrational.

Finally, just very recently in reflecting on the Covid-19 pandemic, the French philosopher and sociologist Edgar Morin (2020) has commented: 'Chaque intelligence individuelle nait de la coopération collective de milliards de neurone, chaque intelligence collective nait de la coopération de nombreux individus' [Each individual intelligence emerges from the collective cooperation of billions of neurons, every collective intelligence emerges from the cooperation of many individuals] (authors' translation).

Note

1 On the concept of '*dividuo*', see Bodei, R. (2013). *Immaginare altre vite. Realtà, progetti, desideri.* Milan: Feltrinelli Editore.

References

Bodei, R. (2013). *Immaginare altre vite. Realtà, progetti, desideri.* Milan: Feltrinelli Editore.

Bozeman, B. (2007). *Public values and public interest: counterbalancing economic individualism.* Washington, DC: Georgetown University Press.

Buchanan, D. (2010). *Playing with fire: the controversial career of Hans Eysenck.* Oxford: Oxford University Press.

Chin, J., & Lin, L. (2022). *Surveillance state: inside China's quest to launch a new era of social control.* New York: St. Martin's Press.

Crane, A., Palazzo, G., Spence, L.J., & Matten, D. (2014). Contesting the value of 'Creating Shared Value'. *California Management Review, 56*(2), 130–53.

Freeman, R.E., Parmar, B.L., & Martin, K. (2020). *The power of and: responsible business without trade-offs.* New York: Columbia University Press.

Gillie, O. (1977). Did Cyril Burt fake his evidence on heritability of intelligence? *Phi Delta Kappan, 58*(6), 469–71.

Mahoney, J.T., McGahan, A.M., & Pitelis, C.N. (2009). Perspective – the interdependence of private and public interests. *Organization Science, 20*(6), 1034–52.

Marks, D. (2019). The Hans Eysenck affair: time to correct the scientific record. *Journal of Health Psychology*, 22 February 2019 (Editorial). Retrieved from https://journals.sagepub.com/doi/10.1177/135910531 8820931, accessed 7 April 2021.

Moore, M. (1995). *Creating public value.* Cambridge: Harvard University Press.

Morin, E. (2020). Citation on Twitter @edgarmorinparis, 8 December 2020. https://twitter.com/edgarmorinparis/status/1234457189001187 329, accessed 7 April 2021.

Normann, R., & Ramírez, R. (1993). From value chain to value constellation: Designing interactive strategy. *Harvard Business Review*, *71*(4), 65–77.

Ostrom E. (1996). Crossing the great divide: coproduction, synergy, and development. *World Development*, *24*(6), 1073–87.

Pasquale, F. (2015). *The black box society: the secret algorithms that control money and information.* Cambridge: Harvard University Press.

Porter, M.E., & Kramer, M. (2011). Creating Shared Value. *Harvard Business Review*, *89*(1), 62–77.

Porter, M.E., & Kramer, M.R. (2014). A response to Andrew Crane et al.'s article. *California Management Review*, *56*, 149–51.

Vargo, S.L., Maglio, P.P., & Akaka, M.A. (2008). On value and value co-creation: a service systems and service logic perspective. *European Management Journal*, *26*(3), 145–52.

Zuboff, S. (2019). *The age of surveillance capitalism: the fight for a human future at the new frontier of power.* New York: Public Affair.

Index

For Product Safety Concerns and Information please contact our EU
representative GPSR@taylorandfrancis.com
Taylor & Francis Verlag GmbH, Kaufingerstraße 24, 80331 München, Germany